Praise for The Wellbeing Curriculum

'Andrew has done it again. An absolutely fabulous book that will help any school to design a curriculum to promote and support the wellbeing of all. A must read for any educator.'
Toria Bono, Primary Teacher and Founder of Tiny Voice Talks

'It is refreshing to read a book that tackles the significance of pupil wellbeing in such an accessible way. The book's attention to wellbeing and character is of particular importance if we want to enable young people to flourish.'
Michael Fullard, Research Fellow at the Jubilee Centre for Character and Virtues, University of Birmingham, @MikeFullard

'*The Wellbeing Curriculum* is a brilliant combination of theory and practical ideas for supporting wellbeing in schools. If you really want to create an environment that embeds wellbeing into the whole school community, this book provides so many areas to explore.'
Dr Hazel Harrison, Clinical Psychologist and Founder of ThinkAvellana, @ThinkAvellana

'Excellent and much-needed, *The Wellbeing Curriculum* is a comprehensive resource, jam-packed with ideas and practical activities to enrich children's lives and support schools with developing a whole school culture of wellbeing.'
Thérèse Hoyle, Author of *101 Playground Games*, Founder of the Positive Playtimes and How to be a Lunchtime Supervisor Superhero programmes

'*The Wellbeing Toolkit* and *The Wellbeing Curriculum* are absolute game-changers and a must-read for anyone working in education.'
John Magee, Author of *Kindness Matters* and *The Happy Tank*

'Andrew captures everything of real importance in education as we redefine the landscape! Read the book, implement the thinking and strategies in your context, deliver a fabulous wellbeing curriculum for your children!'
Adrian McLean, Director of Inclusion, Personal Development & Safeguarding at the Severn Academies Education Trust, @Character_Guy

'As the statutory components of PSHE are consolidated, this excellent book provides welcome support for educational leaders, at all levels, to improve wellbeing and attainment for pupils and staff.'
John Rees, PSHE Trainer and Coach, @PSHESolutions

'With its clear structure, examples, and suggestions for activities and assemblies, *The Wellbeing Curriculum* is a treasure trove for educators wishing to introduce or expand their whole school wellbeing provision.'
Frederika Roberts, School Wellbeing Trainer, Speaker, Author, Lecturer and Founder of Educate to Flourish CIC, @frederika_r and @EduFlourish

'*The Wellbeing Curriculum* is rich with ideas for the primary classroom that are meaningful, practical and innovative. Andrew's passion for wellbeing glows like a beacon of hope throughout and it will be a book that I will turn to again and again.'
Georgina Tait, Primary Teacher, Mental Health First Aider and Director of JustTeachUK

The Wellbeing Curriculum

Embedding children's wellbeing in primary schools

Andrew Cowley

Foreword by Kelly Hannaghan

BLOOMSBURY EDUCATION
LONDON OXFORD NEW YORK NEW DELHI SYDNEY

BLOOMSBURY EDUCATION
Bloomsbury Publishing Plc
50 Bedford Square, London, WC1B 3DP, UK
29 Earlsfort Terrace, Dublin 2, Ireland

BLOOMSBURY, BLOOMSBURY EDUCATION and the Diana logo are trademarks of Bloomsbury Publishing Plc

First published in Great Britain, 2021

A catalogue record for this book is available from the British Library

ISBN: PB: 978-1-4729-8641-2; ePDF: 978-1-4729-8644-3; ePub: 978-1-4729-8642-9

2 4 6 8 10 9 7 5 3 1 (paperback)

Typeset by Newgen KnowledgeWorks Pvt. Ltd., Chennai, India
Printed and bound in the UK by CPI Group Ltd, CR0 4YY

In memory of Janet Lawley.

Teacher. Leader. Inspiration.

Contents

Acknowledgements

This book wouldn't have been possible without the support, dedication and encouragement of a number of people, and I would like to thank the following people for enabling *The Wellbeing Curriculum* to look and read as it does today.

For writing my foreword and for always being a supportive voice of my wellbeing writing, Kelly Hannaghan is a tremendous advocate for wellbeing and a true and trusted friend.

My fellow co-founders of Healthy Toolkit, Maria O'Neill, Helen Dlamini and Matt Young, have always been there with encouraging words and plenty of ideas.

Nicola Owen, Cate Knight and Liz Wright for their thoughts shared in these pages, and Margaret Mizen and Shakira Martin for taking time to be interviewed and for their candid honesty.

Toria Bono for the chance to chat about this book on her podcast; Bethany Eadie at The Key for inviting me to speak to school leaders about building a wellbeing curriculum; Lena Carter and Mal Krishnasamy for the opportunity to talk about this book and *The Wellbeing Toolkit* on Teacher Hug Radio and Teacher Talk Radio respectively.

Bretta Townend-Jowitt for her continued support and advocacy of my first book and encouragement to continue writing this one.

Adrian Bethune for his regular check-ins on my word count.

My friends in the Education Wellbeing collective, in particular Frederika Roberts and Thérèse Hoyle for their encouragement and belief in what is contained in the following pages.

My former colleagues at Orchard Primary School, who have had to listen to me talking about wellbeing for years, and who know how important wellbeing is. Also, a young man who, when I spoke to the children about my first book, asked, 'Mr Cowley, can you write something for us?' Though I cannot share his name, I assured him he would be acknowledged here.

My editor at Bloomsbury, Hannah Marston, for her continued trust and faith in my writing and for her patience and encouragement during the writing process. Also at Bloomsbury, Cathy Lear, Isobel Hawker, Laura Beveridge and Enisha Samra have been a constant source of support and promotion.

For readers wondering about the dedication for this book, Janet Lawley was Vice Principal at my sixth-form college, King George V in Southport. The magic of Twitter is that it shows how connected we are; when Jill Berry, who wrote the foreword to *The Wellbeing Toolkit*, tweeted that Janet Lawley was the best headteacher she had worked for, at Bury Grammar School, another connection was forged. Though Janet didn't teach any of my A level subjects, I was part of her general study groups and knew her well through my parents' involvement in the parent–teacher association. Janet was a teacher of great principle, humour, honesty and integrity, who breathed new life into an institution moving from an all-boys grammar school to a mixed sixth form. It was her example that showed me the value of strong relationships in any school. Just as I received the commission for *The Wellbeing Curriculum*, Jill contacted me to say that Janet had sadly passed away. It is to her memory that this book is dedicated.

This book, as much as the first, would not have been possible without the love, support and patience of my wife Zoé and our daughters Evie and Lily.

Foreword

I am honoured to have been asked to write a few words to introduce this well-crafted and useful book. It has been my pleasure to know Andrew Cowley for a number of years. We were first introduced through the world of Twitter and quickly established a friendship through the alignment in our passion to champion wellbeing in education. I clearly remember my first face-to-face meeting with Andrew. This was on a hot summer's day in the last week of term. Andrew interviewed me in my role as wellbeing lead at my previous primary school. He was interested in exploring how I had successfully led a whole-school approach for wellbeing, creating outstanding outcomes for all stakeholders within the school community. Andrew's findings were later included as a case study in his first book *The Wellbeing Toolkit*.

Andrew impressed me instantly with his rich knowledge and compassionate understanding of what is needed to strategically reshape the way we look at education. I believe he is a trailblazer and is expertly informed to place judgement and guidance on developing a wellbeing-rich curriculum. What Andrew has the courage to do in this book is to challenge our thoughts on the way we set the culture within our schools to support our primary school pupils every day. He offers a vehicle of recovery that prioritises wellbeing as the foundation for learning, along with the key concepts for children to rise from adversity and grow resilience from their experiences of the pandemic.

The Wellbeing Curriculum covers three broad themes for primary-aged children: knowing themselves, knowing others and putting strong values into practice. This book offers a refreshing approach to highlight that every child has their own unique needs and offers reflections through considerations of stepping away from a one-size-fits-all model curriculum for wellbeing.

Andrew highlights the importance of building in the awareness of one's own mental health and strategies for linking to support. This is underpinned by the ideas around developing emotionally intelligent children, who understand and value behaviour, manners and social graces. What is evident in this book is that having meaningful conversations with children about good mental health is underpinned by key statistics that reflect the hurdles educators face in supporting children's wellbeing within the current landscape of education.

It's clear that wellbeing and character education are some of the core features in this book. Take time to ask whether or not your school has these features at the heart of your school curriculum, and if not, then this is the book for you. What I particularly like about this book is how it introduces character as a curriculum itself and how it aims to contribute to well-rounded character development.

Andrew considers the importance of self-awareness, behaviour, manners and conduct. This includes a focus on healthy life choices, care for the environment and personal safety. This book does a great job in offering the tools to help children build their own morals through developing empathy and personal considerations in their life choices.

The Wellbeing Curriculum raises awareness about equality and the fundamental importance of embedding respect for diversity, gender equality, sexuality, identity and disability. These crucial areas of consideration are welcomed in a world of ever-changing approaches to support the needs of all children, in all schools. There is an underlying emphasis on care, kindness and compassion and how these support the basis for securing reciprocal relationships and tackling subjects relating to internet safety and bullying.

I like that there is a focus on friendship issues, as our relationships with others often determine our wellbeing outcomes. This is frequently connected to issues of mental health. What matters is that each child has the opportunity to thrive within their developmental components, then these are most likely to be connected to the thriving development of others.

It's a source of strength that *The Wellbeing Curriculum* explores the direct link to the wellbeing values of Andrew's first book *The Wellbeing Toolkit* and offers a variety of practical strategies that schools might choose to support the emotional development of their pupils through a combination of lesson activities, assembly plans and overall school ethos.

I believe that this book would be a great addition to the commitment and successful implementation of any wellbeing journey. The strategies explored and explained in this book will be conducive to the overall wellbeing of children. These practical guidelines will enable children to flourish on their educational and life journey with a level of skill, knowledge and confidence that will help them to navigate the future.

Kelly Hannaghan
Mental health and wellbeing consultant
@mindworkmatters

Introduction

'The more we are concerned for the well-being of others, the closer we will feel to each other' Dalai Lama XIV (2010)

Wellbeing, in its simplest form, is the absence of disease, but in the reality of twenty-first-century life, it is much more complex than this. Society thrives, or falls, by the quality of the relationships between its members. The connections we have to family, friends and colleagues, to those we love and to those we find more of a challenge, all are determined and shaped by how these relationships form, develop and end.

As our children grow, they develop attachments, and it is the care and sensitivity, feeling and emotion that the subject of their attachment shows in meeting the child's needs that ultimately regulate and control the connectedness that shapes the child's ability to form and maintain positive life relationships in the future. Children form their attachments and build their relationships at home and in their communities as well as in schools, and the manner in which their characters develop and in which their wellbeing is supported will depend on the strength of the triangulation between home, community and school.

Children have a right to wellbeing and to grow up equipped with a range of skills and tools that will enable them to navigate their way through life and to support not only their emotional and mental health, but also their physical, social and economic wellbeing. They also have the right to develop the life skills and qualities that will enable them to support others – in other words, how to become and be a good citizen.

A recent government publication highlighted some important statistics about wellbeing and happiness. The 'State of the Nation 2019: Children and young people's wellbeing' report highlights the challenges that young people face, particularly in reference to age, gender, ethnicity, free school meals (FSM) and special educational needs and disability (SEND) status (Department for Education, 2019a). It draws upon children's feelings about relationships, and about bullying and psychological wellbeing, particularly amongst girls. Whilst this report uses data from children aged ten to 15, from schools in England, it is in the years before the age of ten where I believe we need to set the agenda for wellbeing and good character in the children's school experience.

One of the key statistics is that 84.9 per cent of children, aged ten to 15, report being relatively happy with their lives, but five per cent report being relatively unhappy, and that wellbeing declines as children grow older. There is some evidence that FSM pupils' wellbeing is lower than their non-FSM peers, but both FSM and SEND status are not consistent indicators of poor wellbeing. The wider evidence in the report is that children's overall sense of wellbeing is strengthened, or otherwise, by the experience of different areas of their lives: their happiness with friends, family and school; their experience of bullying; attendance and attainment; and their use of leisure time.

The 'State of the Nation 2019' report concludes with some fundamental themes. Age is important as it is consistently linked with decreasing wellbeing, hence the need to equip children with the necessary skills to support their own, and others', wellbeing in the future. The report also highlights the important differences that children have in their life experiences and how these further impact upon their quality of life. The experience of bullying, including online or cyberbullying, amongst girls in particular, also impacts upon children's emotional health. Whilst all of the above may not be the central factors in impacting wellbeing, they contribute towards it, as too do issues such as loneliness and transition, which are acknowledged as unaddressed in the report. *The Wellbeing Curriculum* seeks to address the themes of this report by considering how primary schools might set out to teach children to look after their own wellbeing and that of others, tackling issues as diverse as respect for the environment, keeping safe online and developing as a young leader, alongside promoting an understanding of good character development.

*

As the concept of this book was becoming more concrete, the world was struck by the Covid-19 pandemic. Pandemics in themselves are a rather obvious threat to wellbeing, but they also offer opportunities for reflection on societal attitudes and for societal change; the Black Death of the fourteenth century, the outbreak of plague in the 1660s and the inaccurately titled Spanish Flu of 1918–1920 led to changes driven by circumstance and necessity, or piloted by those in powerful and influential positions. Whilst major health emergencies are often fuelled by rumour and misinformation, the experience of the spring of 2020 and beyond was powered by 24-hour rolling news and some active or overactive imaginations on social media platforms.

As schools, we shouldn't simply concern ourselves with wellbeing because of the coronavirus and the impacts of lockdown. Effective schools will have been prioritising wellbeing for the whole school community long before this. However, it is apparent that the long-term economic and social impacts of the pandemic will be with us for a substantial period and this is where we need to consider the overarching aim of wellbeing, not as a tick-box exercise or something simply to show the inspectors when they call, but as something that is lived and breathed by the whole school community. Wellbeing was brought into sharper focus during the pandemic, especially after the third lockdown in early 2021, because of the economic and social impact on our children. Economically, families will have faced challenges with working at home, furlough and possible job losses; socially, children have missed their friends and the interactions with adults beyond their families, which, despite the best efforts of parents, are not the same as learning experiences with adults in school.

If, as I developed at length in *The Wellbeing Toolkit*, wellbeing is a strategic consideration for supporting the adults in school, it should be both a pastoral and a curricular consideration for the children. Wellbeing is about mental and physical health. However, if we consider a holistic approach, it is also about life skills and life choices that can impact upon children in the here-and-now, as well as in their long-term future.

The pastoral side of a school will support the children, individually and collectively, through parental liaison, health screening and safeguarding, amongst other aspects of school life. The curricular side of wellbeing, often neglected beyond well-meaning but token days, needs to be embodied through teaching of specific skills and knowledge. Every day needs to be 'Safer Internet Day' because children won't just be online on a Tuesday in February; each week should be 'Mental Health Awareness Week' because, again, the stresses and anxieties that our children experience don't just appear because we teach our children about them. Many of these themes will support or indeed form part of the curriculum: healthy food choices will be a part of science and food technology, for example. Other aspects, such as care for others and for the environment, need to become part of good behaviour choices, whilst earning and showing trust is something to be modelled and practised over time.

About this book

I would firstly like to welcome back readers of *The Wellbeing Toolkit*, which was published by Bloomsbury Education in 2019. When I set out to write my previous book, I realised that *The Wellbeing Toolkit* might stand alone on its own merits, but that it promoted and represented wellbeing for only part of our school community: the staff. In presenting and advocating my first publication, it became apparent that getting wellbeing right for our staff is a precursor to delivery of any meaningful programme of wellbeing for the children. After all, I made the case for effective wellbeing being centred upon relationships and culture within a school. *The Wellbeing Curriculum* can be read as a standalone piece from *The Wellbeing Toolkit*, but I trust that readers who want to make wellbeing a strategic consideration in their schools and trusts, as well as in initial teacher training, might draw upon the principles in both texts.

The Wellbeing Curriculum covers three broad themes for primary-aged children: knowing themselves, knowing others and putting values into practice, the final section being the direct link to the wellbeing values explored in *The Wellbeing Toolkit*. These values underpin a principled approach to staff wellbeing: celebration, collaboration, respect, trust, support, perseverance and resilience, courage, empathy and time. Authentic and ethical school leadership will, by implication, embrace the same values for the whole community. We will look, in *The Wellbeing Curriculum*, at practical ways that schools might choose to support their children through school ethos, assemblies, lesson activities and self-regulation. This is not an 'off-the-shelf' curriculum, because each school, indeed each child, is unique: the 'one size does not fit all' argument from my previous work continues to apply here. I would like this book to be read as a guide to good wellbeing practice in our primary schools.

Our years of experience will have enabled us to help children to build their own moral path through developing empathy and considering the impact of their choices. School leaders may have faced challenges as diverse as a culture of poor behaviour and low expectation, bullying, including cyberbullying, children suffering from self-esteem issues, or perhaps a narrowing of the curriculum, where results are everything and the broader concepts of developing the whole child are relegated by the pressures of accountability. The structure of this book lays out how we might embed wellbeing into our school culture and plans, so that it is there to support all of our children every day of their primary school experience.

The book is split into three broad sections, each building on the other: knowing ourselves, knowing others and putting our wellbeing values into action.

Part 1: Knowing ourselves takes as its starting point that oft-used starter project in Reception of 'Ourselves' but seeks to delve deeper than the children's physical selves into what makes them who they are and who they are going to be. **Chapter 1** discusses the links between wellbeing and character education and establishes why we need to consider wellbeing in its broadest context. **Chapter 2** considers self-awareness, behaviour, manners and conduct, and how we can establish ways of having meaningful conversations with children about good mental health. **Chapter 3** and **Chapter 4** discuss how we might teach healthy life choices, the former relating to the children's own attitudes to healthy eating and exercise, and the latter discussing our children's concern for care for the environment and specifically how we can actively promote this in school. **Chapter 5** concerns teaching awareness of personal safety, particularly in relation to road safety and risky behaviours, as children grow older and become increasingly independent.

Part 2: Knowing others addresses aspects of compassion, kindness and care, and how these build into supporting good relationships in school and beyond. **Chapter 6** discusses how we look after others, friendship issues, bullying and how children can support each other through such experiences. **Chapter 7** specifically addresses e-safety, whilst **Chapter 8** delves deeper into the more challenging area of cyberbullying, how it manifests itself and how we can educate our children to deal with this should they encounter it. **Chapter 9** rounds off this section by debating how we might help to identify, build and maintain trust, whilst also thinking about developing resilience in the face of misplaced trust.

Part 3: Putting wellbeing values into action brings together the themes of the earlier chapters and provides the crux of the message of this book: that wellbeing and life decisions don't stand in isolation and don't sit separately from the academic curriculum but support the development of the whole child. **Chapter 10** takes the theme of representation and leadership beyond a traditional 'give the leadership roles to Year 6' perspective and argues that all children should have the opportunity to develop leadership skills. **Chapter 11** covers respect for diversity, which is always important but has been made more relevant given the events of the summer of 2020, the death of George Floyd and the awareness raised by the campaign of Black Lives Matter. The chapter also includes discussion about gender equality, sexuality and identity, and disability. Finally, **Chapter 12** addresses empowerment, taking the fullest level of responsibility and how we support children in making the best values-led life choices.

This book has been informed, in part, by anonymous survey responses from primary teachers. There were some 300 respondents, and their feedback has been used to inform good practice regarding wellbeing and character, and also to address which areas are perceived as under-resourced or challenging to deal with. Thank you to everyone who added their thoughts. You will find relevant and insightful quotes from some of the respondents highlighted throughout the pages of the book.

How to use this book

The broad themes of 'Knowing ourselves', 'Knowing others' and 'Putting wellbeing values into action' are intended to build upon each other year on year, in the form of a spiral curriculum that enables you to revisit concepts and knowledge as the children's skills, maturity and awareness develop. As readers see the case for wellbeing and character as a curriculum in itself, we will understand that values, leadership skills, mental health awareness and e-safety, for example, are of equal importance for a child in the Early Years as they are for the 11-year-old about to embark upon the journey to secondary school.

I have written also for those professionals who might wish to 'dip into' aspects of wellbeing and character development, and specific chapters and sections have been written to address these. By all means, please pick and choose from the text to support individual aspects of your wellbeing and character development programmes, but remember to consider how wellbeing fits within the development of the whole child.

From Chapter 2 onwards, each chapter includes an example of an assembly that can be adapted for age, audience and context. The chapters also include examples of activities and learning opportunities, complete with links to the National Curriculum where they can be made. These opportunities are divided into Early Years Foundation Stage (EYFS), Key Stage 1, and lower and upper Key Stage 2. EYFS, of course, begins at birth, but for ease of reference in the text, these activities are aimed at nursery and Reception classes. These suggested activities also recognise chances for the children to listen, talk, read and write about their experiences, feelings and reflections.

Slideshows for the assemblies will also be available to download from the dedicated page for this book on the Bloomsbury Education website: bloomsbury.pub/the-wellbeing-curriculum, alongside knowledge organisers for each chapter, which can be downloaded and used with the children in class.

Each chapter ends with a set of success criteria, summarising what good practice looks like for the particular subject being discussed. These criteria can be used as curriculum aims and objectives, which might be built into a school policy document or into your strategic consideration for how to develop an authentic culture of supportive relationships in your school. As I have written before, 'Effective wellbeing is all about relationships and all about culture. About half of what we do in schools is about culture and relationships; the other half is about relationships and culture.' (Cowley, 2019)

PART 1

Knowing ourselves

1 Wellbeing and character education

Chapter overview

This opening chapter sets the case for wellbeing and character education as part of the curriculum and as a curriculum in themselves.

Areas discussed

Wellbeing and character education are natural partners, not in the sense of being 'soft' subjects, but in terms of the ways in which they can support the core structure of the education of the whole child as an individual, as a member of society and as a global citizen. This, I believe, represents a broader view of what defines 'success' for our children.

Many believe that character education, as much as a wellbeing curriculum, needs to be at the heart of the culture, values and vision of the school. In her LeAF (Learn and Flourish) model, Frederika Roberts places academic attainment, staff and student wellbeing, and a wellbeing curriculum, as elements of whole-school positive and character education, supported by roots including culture and relationships (Roberts, 2020). Though we all wish our children to perform well academically, the wealth of their education will be gained from being able to thrive in life and add to the wellbeing of their communities. By taking a whole-school approach to character and wellbeing development, beginning from Early Years, we can prepare children for a life journey that will see them engage the core values that will make them empathetic adults. In doing so, teachers will need to exemplify and communicate the most positive character traits in the ways they interact with their pupils, families and other stakeholders.

Defining wellbeing for children

Wellbeing is about physical and mental health, and within this definition will fall human happiness. However, is there more to life than happiness? Adrian Bethune and I have discussed this often, and Adrian outlines the differences between subjective and psychological wellbeing: one's own assessment of what life satisfaction is, as opposed to a sense of meaning and purpose in life (Bethune, 2018). Individual actions, events or accomplishments might make us happy: a funny joke, an amusing cat video, sporting success for a favourite team or individual. The impact of such may be instantaneous and short-lived. It is the belief of some positive psychologists that happiness and meaning sustain each other (Seligman, 2011) and that the search for happiness accompanies the search for meaning in life (Baumeister, 1992). Happiness, in the truest sense, is long-term, sustained and lifelong.

Wellbeing in school isn't a tick-box exercise, for adults or children, nor should it be compartmentalised as 'happiness lessons' separate from the rest of the children's learning. If we are going to seriously consider wellbeing as part of the curriculum, we need to place it where it will nourish and nurture, challenge and confront, extend and enlarge the educational and life experiences of our children. It must underpin, not undermine, the wider curriculum and teaching and learning as a whole.

Wellbeing is empathetic and honest

As teachers, we all wish to ensure that our pupils go on to lead accepting, caring, successful and safe futures. An empathetic classroom is the potential breeding ground for this, provided that the adults before the class model empathy for the children. Consistent modelling of empathy, in dealing with the day-to-day minutiae of the classroom, as well as the challenges arising from behaviour and fallings-out, enables children to develop genuine feelings of trust in their adults. The classroom should be a place to acknowledge mistakes, to discuss feelings and emotions, and to build them into the learning process.

The classroom and playground may become the places where children have their first introduction outside of the family to those of a different gender, race, faith or age, through the people they meet and by the learning experiences they have. This initial educational encounter with diversity and difference is essential to the development of meaning and purpose in life.

Wellbeing is collective

Teamwork is at the core of good staff wellbeing, so should apply equally to children too. 'Tribal classrooms', with their collective spirit often indicated by 'class flags' (Bethune, 2018), demonstrate a positive bond in the primary classroom. I have taught some great classes, and the very best of these have shown a sense of team spirit in both their attitude to learning and academic progress, but also in the ways in which they support each other. Building from the empathetic and honest classroom, and the strength of community outside of school, a class of 30 children can be a force for good: in their relationships with each other, the ways in which they stand up for their friends and the ways in which they challenge perceived injustices. My classes that have performed best academically have always had the strength of collaboration behind them. I don't believe they would have achieved so much without this.

Wellbeing is routine

Children thrive on routine. It brings comfort and consistency, security and self-discipline. Life, of course, isn't consistent, and change is a part of life that needs to be built into a child's learning experience. Having a regular routine, as any parent will attest to from domestic experience, is essential to the smooth running of any primary classroom, creating a familiar pattern of key events during each day and through the week.

Wellbeing can be built into this routine, whether it manifests itself in mindfulness activities or in managing behaviour and reward. Routine and consistent use of the behaviour management policy, both for reward and sanction, are important for a sense of calm and purpose in the classroom; where behaviour isn't well-managed, relationships in class can become fragile and challenging. The most successful teachers don't need to raise their voices; the most trusting children build that trust through the knowledge that rules and reward will be applied fairly and consistently.

Routine is also fundamental to good learning, providing the security and confidence that children know what is expected of them in their work in lessons and behaviour, both within and outside the classroom. If they are unsure, uncertainty creeps in, which is not conducive to good emotional health. Regular repeated language, in a meaningful social context, embeds that language in the memory and encourages its active use. Turn-taking, predictable and familiar skills, the building of confidence and a sense of responsibility: each supports the development of a sense of community and builds social and emotional skills. Routines bring confidence and reassurance, which are both at the heart of the wellbeing development that our young children need.

Wellbeing is part of good relationships and school culture

Without good relationships, there is no supportive culture in any workplace. In a school, poor relationships in the working environment are difficult enough for staff to deal with and are soon detected by the children. Without good staff wellbeing, there is little hope for the children's happiness and emotional health. In our positive culture, the wellbeing values I have written of previously (celebration, collaboration, respect, trust, support, perseverance and resilience, courage, empathy and time) apply equally to children as much as to the adults they work with.

A commitment to wellbeing needs to be in the ethos of the primary school and be apparent from the moment the children arrive in the Early Years Foundation Stage (EYFS) and continue until their rite of passage to secondary school. The expectations of behaviour, and how it is managed and rewarded, together with how the children work and play with one another, are essential components of the social skills that they need to progress through life. Children will arrive with different experiences, backgrounds, language development and other needs, but on their first entry to school we can start to furnish them with consistent values and morals within the culture the school embodies. Through assemblies, conduct in the corridors and the playground, interactions with teaching assistants and midday staff, as well as their experiences in the classroom with their teacher, children will be exposed to many positive encounters. These influences, consistently applied, will determine the positive culture that we would wish our children to experience.

The place of character education alongside wellbeing

There is nothing new about 'character education', either in a British or in a global context. Character and virtues date back to the likes of Aristotle and Confucius, and beyond. From the latter half of the twentieth century, character education has fitted the agendas of world leaders, be they in a revolutionary socialist republic or in a more politically conservative society reacting to perceived societal difficulties:

> *'The equal right of all citizens to health, education, work, food, security, culture, science, and wellbeing – that is, the same rights we proclaimed when we began our struggle, in addition to those which emerge from our dreams of justice and equality for all inhabitants of our world – is what I wish for all.' Fidel Castro Ruz (2015)*
>
> *'The future success of our Nation depends on our children's ability to understand the difference between right and wrong and to have the strength of character to make the right choices. To help them reach their full potential and live with integrity and pride, we must teach our children to be kind, responsible, honest, and self-disciplined. These important values are first learned in the family, but all of our citizens have an obligation to support parents in the character education of our children.'*
> *George W. Bush (2002)*

Whilst Castro's revolution may not have reached all levels of society as planned – except for in education, where the national literacy rate reached 96 per cent (Kellner, 1989) – and the younger Bush played perhaps to the vision of the 'American Dream', there is much in these contrasting political beliefs that is remarkably similar. Each is focused on values: justice and equality; kindness and responsibility. They each emphasise ambition, be it dreams or future success. Both also highlight the message, by reference to *'all (our) citizens'*, that there is a collective responsibility to achieve these goals.

In England, the Jubilee Centre for Character and Virtues advocates the development of character education in schools, with an emphasis on good moral character and moral integrity having a positive impact upon life and learning. In investigating how young people dealt with moral dilemmas and how teachers viewed the promotion of moral character, their 2015 report found that 80 per cent of teachers interviewed felt that the current system of assessment hindered the development of 'the whole child'. Thirty-three per cent had received no training in teaching moral or character education (Arthur et al., 2015). In the same year, the then Secretary of State for Education, Nicky Morgan, launched the Character Education Awards. Twenty-seven schools won a prize for their work in character education, with an emphasis on developing resilience and grit.

The drive for a place for character was given further impetus by the more recent publication of the framework guidance for character education (Department for Education, 2019b). Whilst non-statutory, the guidance discusses the rationale behind character education and the practicalities of embedding it within a school culture. Here the complex nature of character is recognised, but a central point is the long-term view, as opposed to instant reward and gratification, and the ability to deal with disappointment and perceptions of failure. A moral commitment to faith, vocation, personal relationships and the wider community is also emphasised. Values, not 'British' values but universal virtues, such as honesty and a sense of justice, also have a place, alongside respect for the opinions of others. The ability to deal with those who may have a different opinion, to listen, to persuade and to be well-mannered is also covered within this broad definition.

The Department for Education guidance lays out six character benchmarks, summarising what schools developing character might consider. How might wellbeing fit alongside the benchmarks detailed below?

Character benchmark 1: What kind of school are we?

Does the school clearly convey a sense of pride and belonging? Are children, parents and staff pleased to be part of this learning community?

In defining what kind of education the school wishes to provide, whether the school takes a knowledge-rich or a more discovery learning outlook, if the school defines clearly the values and community spirit, then a bedrock for the whole school character is in place. Academic progress is important to life chances, but alongside this the school needs to develop its expectations; we would all like to see a well-qualified dentist or lawyer, construction worker or IT technician, but in dealing with them we would hope they demonstrate manners, social graces and honesty. The place to make these habitual is at primary school.

Reward and recognition are one means of expressing a sense of pride, and the manner and means of reward and of achievement define our schools too. Reward may be given simply for schoolwork or for a combination of other aspects of school life. Are the rewards you give meaningful or tokenistic and do they receive the full public recognition they deserve?

Wellbeing in such schools will reflect the culture and relationships in the school as the sense of pride will be reflected in the positive and polite interactions every child and adult has with every other member of the school community.

Character benchmark 2: What are our expectations of behaviour towards each other?

By behaviour, we need to look at much more than behaviour policy, rewards and sanctions, rules and expectations, and how they are applied. Behaviour policies are only as good as the teacher and senior leader putting them into practice. The teacher who uses no other strategies apart from the behaviour policy will find managing a class a challenge; the senior leader who doesn't follow through on consequences appears unsupportive of their colleague.

Children need to understand that rules are there so they feel safe and secure, but is this articulated to them? Do conversations about behaviour focus on reward or punishment? Behaviour systems focused on keeping the children 'in line' may not, in their wording, promote good manners, respect for others or consideration and empathy for the feelings of others. There is a huge difference in the impact of rules beginning with *'Do...'* and those beginning *'Do not...'* and it would be of interest to see how many lists of rules include the words 'please' and 'thank you' within individual rules or in the accompanying text.

Behavioural expectations in a school promoting good character will proactively promote the essential character traits that we wish to see in our young people. The collective responsibility and routine nature of good behaviour link this character trait to firm wellbeing foundations.

Character benchmark 3: Resilience and confidence

The guidance specifically references 'cultural capital', a term that seems abstract and imprecise. The phrase doesn't necessarily refer to class visits to the opera and to art galleries, which some children will have experience of but many won't for any number of societal, economic and geographical reasons. This provides a very narrow definition of what 'culture' is. Rather, culture is manifested in the knowledge, attitudes, behaviours and skills that the children can draw upon in the ways that they contribute to their communities. Culture will come from the experiences determined for them through their curriculum and the strength of their academic progress and personal confidence. In my teaching experience, a child may be inspired by a theatre visit in the power of communication through the spoken word and facial expression; equally, a more down-to-earth visit to a local care home to be taught to play dominoes by two elderly residents may also encourage the children to converse effectively in a different context.

The effective curriculum will then allow the children to use the skills and knowledge they acquire and to apply them in the decisions they make. In Chapters 10 to 12 of this book, we will see how the logically sequenced aspects of wellbeing skills and knowledge can become part of the wider curriculum experience and be integrated into teaching and learning.

Resilience, more specifically mental resilience, sometimes referred to as 'grit', is built in any number of ways. Displays entitled *'Be the best that you can be'* or similar will be familiar to many primary colleagues, but without building this message into the curriculum experience of the children, these can appear hollow. This could emerge from developing a growth mindset, as opposed to a fixed one, encouraging the children that they can achieve with application and effort. Equally, where there is an ethos of reflection, of drawing upon and learning from mistakes, in learning or in conduct, children have the opportunity to employ this essential life skill. They can develop self-reflection, but of equal worth are the appreciation of feedback from peers and the acquisition of positive habits and attitudes from others.

Character benchmark 4: The quality of the co-curriculum

In terms of the wider curriculum, that part of school life that isn't covered by the National Curriculum, religious education or assemblies, what do we provide? Schools with high numbers of children classed as 'disadvantaged' and in receipt of the Pupil Premium may have allocated some of this funding stream to invest in resources, human or otherwise, but equally may have leant on the knowledge, expertise and enthusiasm of their staff.

Sports are always popular choices, football in particular, but do we use such ventures to build character as much as sporting prowess? The ability to accept defeat with dignity, to show a sense of fair play and respect for the decisions of officials – many readers who have run school football clubs may recognise the challenges in instilling these values at times, but the sport does embrace community involvement, particularly through the other programmes that professional clubs offer. The celebration of success doesn't necessarily mean the winning of trophies and medals, but recognition of team and individual effort.

Rugby or the martial arts are both examples of sports with strong moral codes built into the way they are played, which are also positive examples of promoting character development. The use of trained staff and high-quality provision brings a level of skill progress that eagerness alone may not develop as fully.

The enthusiasm that our colleagues show for interests that they wish to share with the children provides an ideal opportunity to grow children's curiosity outside the classroom setting. By way of example, I have seen colleagues lead after-school clubs in such diverse activities as stop-frame animation, ballroom dancing and ukulele, as well as the more traditional primary school pursuits of choir, recorders, dance and drama. The provision of such opportunities and the chance to share and celebrate, by a drama production or a fruit and vegetable show, for example, shows there is purpose and depth in such enterprises.

Wellbeing and character development have a firm place in the co-curriculum, sports and the rest of the broader curriculum, offering wider opportunities to demonstrate an empathetic mindset as well as a sense of collective responsibility as a team member or as an individual contributing to the greater good of everyone.

Character benchmark 5: Volunteering and service to others

In the primary school, such activities would need much supervision and appropriate risk assessment for reasons of safeguarding, but opportunities to support the local community in a voluntary capacity can be meaningful and establish relationships between the school and local business and charities. Rather than one-off events, these opportunities can be built into annual routines. The choir singing at the local care home is probably well established; the Harvest Festival contributions going to the local food bank may be a newer experience. In both examples, there is a plethora of opportunity to build civic-minded conduct and to break down social barriers. With food banks in particular, there is the ideal occasion to challenge the stigma that is sometimes associated with such institutions.

Volunteering in the community is a means also to boost parental engagement. During the pandemic, many of us were delighted to receive pictures of our families delivering food parcels and medicines to the doorsteps of elderly and vulnerable neighbours. This may not have been a response to the circumstances of the time, but a value ingrained in the psyche of our children through the ethos of their school, one perhaps that emphasises the common good over the needs of the individual.

The notion of service to others has a place within the school setting too. As will be seen in Chapter 10, the way we encourage children to take responsibility and to act as leaders can go beyond the usual pencil monitor and school council roles to duties that may be less prominent in the eyes of peers but of equal or greater value to character development.

The idea of being a 'Junior Citizen' is promoted in many schools and local authorities, often accompanied by prizes and public recognition. The importance of recognition and reward in character education needs to be balanced with the recognition that not every action brings extrinsic reward, but that there is a value in less material terms in developing a sense of personal reward and satisfaction. This sense of pride, of empathy and of doing good for goodness's sake alone links back to the earlier definitions of wellbeing.

Character benchmark 6: Does every child benefit equally from the offer?

Dig down below the surface and we find that no two schools are the same. Communities and catchments contrast, even with schools within walking distance of each other. Within each school, classes will differ, often reflecting upon changes within the community: new housing (both social or owner-occupied), transport links, job opportunities and local economic fortunes can all affect the composition of the school roll. These differences could act as barriers to participation, in terms of parental support, background, financial costs, location and distances to travel. Does your school enable all your children to feel that they belong, to feel valued and to be challenged?

Genuine equality of opportunity and of access to everything the school has to offer matches the agenda of wellbeing and character education, wellbeing being for everyone and where honesty and empathy form part of our children's development. However, in enabling every child to access this aspect of learning fairly, we will need to apply the same principles that we do to meet the needs of our disadvantaged pupils elsewhere in the curriculum: the child we support in reading and in mathematics might require a similar degree of support in being able to access our teaching of character. Equally, though, this child may not need this support, but perhaps a child with social and economic advantages, through not demonstrating great empathy for their peers, may benefit from more scaffolded and directed lessons in this element of our curriculum.

Wellbeing and character as curriculum

Curriculum isn't simply what we teach between the hours of nine and three. It is not simply reading, writing and spelling; arithmetic and geometry; history and music. Curriculum in other words is not the National Curriculum plus religious education. Curriculum is not just a body of knowledge, because if it is, and we teach our children nothing else, then are we building our leaders, our teachers and health care professionals, our technicians and artists of the future?

Of course, we don't just teach our children a volume of knowledge. We enable them to access and use that knowledge through a range of learning skills, through modelling and scaffolding, repetition and reinforcement. Then we test them.

There is more to education than tests and there is more to the school day than lesson times. Every interaction the children have with each other, with their teacher and teaching assistant, with other adults and children at break and dinner time – these all form part of their learning experience. Their curriculum should be one in which they will use the life skills of communication and negotiation, kindness and empathy, compassion and collaboration, wellbeing and character.

In the pages that follow, I will set out the case for a wellbeing and character curriculum that will sit alongside, within and astride the purely academic curriculum, and I will argue that, although this cannot be quantifiable in the same way as examination data, it is the most important part of what we teach our young people for their, and our, futures.

Success criteria: What does a school that prioritises wellbeing and character education look like?

- Empathy and honesty feature prominently in the wellbeing on offer to the whole school community.
- Teamwork and a bond of collective responsibility is promoted through every aspect of school life.
- Wellbeing is built into the routine of the school, for every day and for every stakeholder: child, parent, governor, teacher and support staff.
- Wellbeing feeds the excellent working relationships and positive culture of the school.
- Your character education offer defines the school in which you wish your pupils to learn and experience in their primary years.
- Character drives excellent behaviour, which in turn enables relationships to thrive.
- Children will learn to be resilient, and to grow in self-confidence and in the ability to reflect.
- Character and wellbeing support, and are supported by, the wider curriculum on offer.
- Children will have a sense of pride in and duty towards their community.
- The wellbeing and character curriculum will be equally available to all your pupils.

2 Self-awareness

Chapter overview

This chapter sets out the case for linking wellbeing and character across the entire primary phase. We will discuss how we might teach and embed core aspects of wellbeing and character. These are essential elements that will underpin the themes through this book and be echoed in the final chapter and its focus on authentic values that support life choices.

Areas discussed

Learning opportunities and activities

Assembly theme

When our children enter school for the first time, the classic EYFS topic or project 'Ourselves' might represent the first part of their more formalised learning journey. Perhaps these days covered in more creatively titled formats such as 'Me, Myself and I' or 'Me and My Community', the basic tenets remain the same: that the children are unique and special, how important friendship and family are, and how, as they expand their horizons beyond home, the school and the community are there to help them.

When they arrive with us in nursery and Reception classes, for many children this is their first break from the familiar. The boundaries of home, immediate and extended family, and the warmth and security that these provide, are, for the next few hours at least, removed. This transition, as any EYFS practitioner will attest to, can vary on a scale from seamless to highly emotional as the 'ourselves' who arrive with us have experienced a diverse learning journey already. Some will not have experienced playgroup or attended nursery and will not have had the range of social interactions that some of their peers will have experienced. For every child with a rich vocabulary for their age, exposed to language through talk and sharing stories and books, there will be others to whom this experience is much less familiar. There will be children who run happily into class in September with high levels of confidence and others who cling nervously to their parents' hands and need an amount of coaxing into their new setting.

The Reception baseline assessment, compulsory from September 2021 but already trialled by early adopter schools, which is based on the children's starting points in language, communication and literacy as well as mathematics, will be used as a school progress measure in Year 6. Whilst no numerical value will be attached, a series of narrative statements result, informing teachers of a child's performance at the time. By 2028, providing no changes occur in the interim, the first judgements will result, based on this assessment and the Key Stage 2 SATs of that year.

From arrival, our practitioners will always assess their new charges as to their 'baseline' or starting point. Whilst there will be an evaluation of the numerical and communication skills the child has, so too will there be an analysis of their social skills, interactions with adults and children, and their capacity to engage in play, with materials and with the natural world. It is these aspects of the wider learning experience that ultimately shape our children as much as their fledgling academic showing.

Some of us who were teaching in the first decade of this century may recall the 2009 Independent Review of the Primary Curriculum, otherwise known as 'The Rose Review' after Sir Jim Rose CBE, chair of the advisory group and a former director of inspection at Ofsted. One of the core recommendations was that children be taught not only *what* to study but *how* to study and learn, and thus to become confident, self-disciplined and engaged in learning. Crucially, it also recommended closer links between EYFS and Years 1 to 6, dovetailing the then six broad areas of learning into the Key Stage 1 and 2 curriculum. Though the review was never actioned, being shelved by the coalition government in 2010, those principles of linking the areas of learning across the primary years justify the themes of this book, drawing as they do upon themes applicable across the three to 11 age range. 'Ourselves', broadened into self-awareness, represents the starting point for the wellbeing and character curriculum, because knowing ourselves is the root from which, living and breathing, the wellbeing experience can grow.

Mental health awareness

I'm not going to pretend for one minute that this book will cover anywhere near everything that we might wish to achieve in a mentally healthy school. Other publications will cover this in far greater detail than I am able to. However, starting with a degree of self-awareness can enable our young children to begin on their educational and life journey with a level of skill, knowledge and confidence that will help them to navigate the challenges ahead.

If we are able to teach children how to understand their feelings – how they might feel if they are excited, surprised, hopeful, disappointed, worried or anxious – then we set them on a path where they can have feelings but they can talk openly about how they manage their emotions and worries in a place where they are neither judged nor judge each other.

Being self-aware will also enable children to feel good about themselves, without feeling self-conscious. It may also encourage them to be prepared to take risks – not dangerous risks, but ones in which the learning isn't stifled by the simple fear of making mistakes, a reflection that mirrors the thoughts of the psychologist Lev Vygotsky (1978). In simple terms, the zone of proximal development (ZPD) can be represented diagrammatically by three circles within each other. The central circle represents what the child can do unaided, the outer one what the child cannot do and the other circle being the ZPD, representing what a child will be able to do with expert guidance and eventually be able to complete independently. Expanding the boundary of the ZPD, pushing fear of failure to the back of the mind, allows the child to be fearless and to try new experiences and adventures. To help our children in expanding their ZPD and managing their feelings, by giving strategies to help them relax, such as mindfulness and meditation, they can be helped to cope with anxiety. Self-awareness can also help children to stand up for themselves, to be politely assertive and to stand by their views and opinions.

To be supportive of mental health, schools need to develop a culture in which children and adults alike are able to feel comfortable in discussing how they feel. In other words, we need to create talking and listening schools. If this is built into the school culture, it will become obvious, beyond having posters announcing 'We are a talking school' or a brightly labelled 'listening' bench, which may look attractive but is little used. If we are serious about attaining a good standard for emotional health and wellbeing, schools should demonstrate openly how they address such issues, so that children understand what they are feeling and to enable them to build their confidence to learn.

This is where wellbeing and character lie not only within but also alongside a traditional view of classroom learning, because very often issues such as emotional wellbeing may arise in class but also at playtimes, when socialising with friends and at times spent with adults other than their class teacher. From their first experience in school, children can be taught that their behaviour can affect other people, both children and adults, and that listening to other people has a positive impact on their perception and how they are perceived by others. As children enter Key Stage 2 and other factors such as hormones come into play, specific teaching of how emotions change as we physically grow can also assist children and how they deal with their feelings in a more challenging environment.

Here also lies an opportunity to address the consequences of antisocial and aggressive behaviours, such as bullying or racism. In addition, teachers might think about the different risks that children can put themselves in, which often become very apparent as they get older. This can include making judgements about kinds of physical contact that may or may not be appropriate.

Mental health in the 2020s: the place of emotional intelligence

Our young people have lived and indeed are still living through momentous times. Global events that impact upon adults will have a different interpretation from a child's point of view. A pandemic, which has created uncertainty, fear and isolation, a seemingly daily diet of fake news and hyperbole, and the challenge to values such as the rule of law and respect for democracy, in, at the very least, a disrespectful, and at worst violent, manner – these are difficult enough for an adult to comprehend and bewildering for many of our children. Consider also that many of our children will have seen the video of the last moments of George Floyd, which may have triggered memories of prior trauma for some children and frightened others. Such disturbing global events, as much as the children's own experiences, can have a significant impact on the mental health of our primary school pupils.

We all have mental health, in the same way we all have physical health. On some days we will feel resilient, on other days less so. Mental health isn't something that develops in adulthood; its root causes lie in childhood experience. In fact, more than half of all adult mental health problems start before the age of 14 (Kessler et al., 2005).

The role of schools in supporting positive mental health is twofold: firstly, in creating a protective environment that serves to prevent everyday stresses from becoming more serious problems; secondly, in developing a robust system to identify and refer to interventions when mental health difficulties are disrupting developmental progress and healthy functioning. Children in the primary sector spend half their waking hours in school, so as a community hub, our role has never been as important.

One teacher in my research survey commented on what worked well for creating such a protective environment:

> *'Being honest and open. Be prepared to talk about your own (appropriate) experiences. Talk about what did and didn't work for you. Let children know it's OK not to be OK. Talk about what you might be feeling, like if you need to seek help.'*

Some of our children may have experienced bereavement and, in the pandemic, the heartache of not being able to visit their loved ones or to say goodbye. For others, the simple pleasure of being with friends and family has been taken from them; this too is a form of grief and should not be underestimated. The nature and longevity of these friendships are quite naturally going to have been altered by the lack of proximity; the contact offered through a digital platform is no substitute for the concrete nature of friendship grown through proximity.

Encouraging children to think about their feelings, to talk about them and to be open in expressing their hopes, fears and aspirations is important for a number of reasons:

- Recognition and understanding of their own feelings enable children to become more self-aware. Being able to do so without judgement can allow children to become truly reflective.
- When feelings can be thought about, children are less likely to engage in acting out or speaking out their behaviours.
- Comprehension of their own emotions and feelings means that children are more likely to empathise with other children and with adults.
- Empathy is at the very heart of developing good relationships.
- Children rely on adults, at home and at school, to co-regulate strong feelings. Supporting the child to understand their feelings, easing upset and helping them to return to a state of calm can all support this regulation.
- Emotional literacy can develop children's resilience and perseverance: how they deal with difficulties and maintain good mental health. Emotional literacy represents one step towards the development of emotional intelligence.

If we consider the work of Daniel Goleman on the subject, we find that emotional intelligence is considered to be of greater importance than intellectual intelligence. In fact, Goleman suggested that intellectual intelligence is responsible for only 20 per cent of success in education and the workplace (Goleman, 1995). If then the balance lies with emotional intelligence, is this not a case for wellbeing and character within the curriculum? Goleman lists five components of emotional intelligence, each of which supports the principles of a wellbeing curriculum:

- **Self-awareness:** the ability to recognise and understand our own emotions and drivers and the effect they have on others. It may involve taking a moment to stop and 'check in' with oneself. The practice of mindful meditation can facilitate this.
- **Self-regulation:** control or redirection of disruptive impulses and moods. This can include not acting judgmentally and thinking before speaking out or acting upon an occurrence. Trust, integrity, adapting to ambiguity and openness to change are associated with strong self-regulation.
- **Internal motivation:** thinking beyond external rewards and being driven by our own goals, values and curiosities. Optimistic people often show strong internal motivation.
- **Empathy:** more than simply listening, empathy is about understanding the emotional foundations of others. Empathetic people are skilled in recognising and promoting talent and in being culturally sensitive.
- **Social skills:** the ability to make and grow relationships, the knowledge of how to talk to people and how to conduct oneself in different situations.

All five of these components, if we have them as adults in school, enable us to work with our colleagues, manage change and, most importantly, look after ourselves. For the children, developing their emotional intelligence will be a foundation stone of their future success but will require learning and practice; it needs to be taught, not caught.

Nicola Owen is a trained teacher, wellbeing practitioner and founder of Zennic Wellbeing, which supports children, parents and staff in a range of wellbeing services. On the following page, Nicola has kindly shared her thoughts on the importance of talk for supporting mental health.

The power of talk on mental health, by Nicola Owen

'It's good to talk' was a well-coined phrase spoken by Bob Hoskins during the mid-1990s for a very prominent telecommunications company in England. He wasn't wrong. The power of talk on improving mental health has long been a tool in addressing many mental health illnesses. The use of cognitive behavioural therapy (CBT), counselling, behavioural activation, interpersonal therapy (IPT) and eye movement desensitisation and reprocessing (EMDR) therapy are all recognised talking therapies designed to treat a multitude of mental health conditions.

What if the power of talking could serve as a preventative technique to avoid negative mental health conditions from developing?

You have heard the proverb 'A problem shared is a problem halved.' Talking about how we feel, our emotions, helps to develop our emotional intelligence. Starting from a very young age, our behaviours tend to demonstrate how we are feeling, rather than words. As we follow modelled behaviours from the grown-ups around us, we hopefully learn how to process our emotions, and express them through words, in a way that doesn't cause us harm or develop into mental health conditions.

Giving our young people the time and a safe space to talk in a busy world is crucial. Giving time to sit and be with one another, share stories, build connections and show our vulnerabilities all help in building those positive connections that support the act of talking and listening. Communicating to support positive mental health is a proactive tool in combating further mental health conditions developing further down the line. It's good to talk.

The teaching of behaviour

The 'teaching' of behaviour is easier said than done. Whilst there is a school of thought that calls for a sanction for every misdemeanour to be punished and another that says that 'all behaviour is communication', the reality of primary school is that the main issue we have with conduct is low-level disruption, talking and calling out, with the occasional outburst of pushing and shoving on the playground. It is less common, though not unknown, for more serious breaches of behaviour rules to occur; here, though, the discussion is about establishing and embedding a culture of high standards of behaviour and motivating the children to meet this expectation.

Behaviour is more than 'must' and 'must not', and in the same way as 'be kind', this means little to a child who has not had this modelled for them. 'Be good' will be equally meaningless without concrete examples of what 'being good' looks like. A more appropriate terminology for adults would be the setting of high expectations because this is the bar that ideally we set from EYFS and maintain consistently, with adjustments for their growing maturity, through to the end of Year 6.

Consistency will always be the key to any good behaviour management strategy. If a child knows exactly where they stand if they behave well or if they break a rule, there is no element of surprise. Consistency is key to developing good character, as is the response to poor behaviour. As teachers, we are employed and paid to impart skills and knowledge. Our time is precious and finite. We will all be faced with some poorer behaviour each day but dealing with it simply, fairly and quickly will allow us the time to teach. Explaining that the behaviour is a breach of the rules and what the sanction is takes seconds and allows us to move the lesson along seamlessly. A lengthy rebuke that the whole class, or the class next door, can hear only serves to impact on learning time and crucially shows the child that they have 'won' in annoying the teacher and drawing negative attention to themselves. Similarly, lengthy enquiries into individual but trivial incidents serve only to waste valuable teacher time (often that of a senior leader) and keep a child away from learning.

By turning negativity on its head, by not taking time out of learning time and instead paying positive attention to good behaviour and to correct choices, we can instantly change the mood and culture of a room. By knowing that the adult will focus on what constitutes good behaviour and recognises it, the child will see that they receive the attention they deserve rather than the child doing the incorrect thing. In terms of character, promotion of good behaviour also advocates that this is something to be proud of, not to be embarrassed about.

Reward systems similarly need to reflect this positive mindset. A daily and ongoing reward totaliser, for which a number of online applications are available, acknowledges, at the touch of a screen, good work in learning and behaviour and also feeds this information back to parents. Such apps can also inform the parents of behaviour breaches, and this needs consideration as a school, particularly as parents would rather be informed of misdemeanour through a conversation, rather than via an impersonal notification on their phone. In my school, we did away with this side of the application, having seen a sea of red on a few class charts. Taking away rewards already earned is demoralising for the child and an annoyance for the parent. If a child has broken a rule, one serious enough for parents to know, then the parent will appreciate a call or a conversation at the gate; forgetting their homework or calling out needs dealing with in class, nothing more. Every negative interaction needs something like eight positive ones to create a sense of balance. If the child complains that a teacher is always telling them off, the parent receiving a notification of each one will have some reason to believe them; the one who knows that consistent behaviour management doesn't need such an approach will rest more assured.

Reward systems also rely on simplicity to be effective. The daily rewards may build to a weekly, monthly or termly total and may be acknowledged in a celebration assembly. This may also be the place to recognise individual pieces of great work in a whole school and community setting. Parents love to see their child receiving an award and recognition for their achievements, however small. Of course, there is the pride in being the star of the week or year and of lifting a trophy to go with it, but never underestimate the power of a positive phone call home or a quick word at afternoon pick-up. Parents very much appreciate the efforts made by teachers for taking the time that such calls require. It is upon these interactions that the positive relationships with parents can build and thrive.

Parents and children alike can also see through systems that are perhaps contrived and unfair. If a school has a system where there are a limited number of certificates each week and a tick-list to ensure that every child receives one each term, teachers will be left scratching their heads about what to award a particular child and will be on the receiving end of children's incredulous looks when a peer who has been challenging in some way is rewarded at the end of the week. One of the most liberating innovations we put in place at my school was to rid ourselves of the two certificates a week limit and to give awards authentically and honestly. The incentive for the children who might not receive an award comes from the sight of their peers being recognised, and the motivation for the teacher is to recognise good achievement and to ensure they really know their children. This way, we ensure that every child is rewarded, not because it is 'their turn', but because they deserve it for their work, conduct and character.

The Friday celebration assembly, by whichever name it goes in school, needs to be a core part of the week, celebrating the fact that the school is part of the community. How often do we remember that a component of the word 'community' is 'unity'? Standing together as a school – children, parents and teachers – demonstrates the value that the institution places upon good conduct and character, the pride that children and parents have in this achievement and sharing of high expectation by everyone. For every argument that this eats into learning time, we also need to consider that the assembly might be the only opportunity that children have to witness and share what is going on in other classrooms or to meet children from other year groups and see consistency in action. Hosting assemblies as an online meeting represents another means of sharing the same principles in more challenging times.

One of the most impactful rewards in my school has been Hot Chocolate Friday, popularised by Paul Dix's writing, but when introduced at our school in response to pupil voice, one eloquent young man pointed out that, 'Some of us are well behaved all the time, but there are children who get a reward for turning up at school.' We launched Hot Chocolate Friday with no fanfare at first, just letting the message seep out slowly. We now announce the winners in our Friday Celebration Assembly and select one child from each class. A deserving member of staff gets a hot chocolate too!

They all love the special mugs and the low-calorie hot chocolate, but the real impact is for those children who might previously have only been to the head's room for a sanction. They talk about their week, they ask us all sorts of questions they wouldn't dare ask in class, they laugh and joke and pose for a photograph with their mugs, which is posted on the Hot Choc Friday tab of our website. Schools are founded on good relationships and this simple initiative, which takes little effort, has helped these to grow.

Teaching good manners

The teaching of good manners is not something that can be covered in lessons alone, if they can be taught as lessons at all. Arguably, the teaching of manners can only come through the setting of examples: holding a door open, the correct use of cutlery, answering a question with due courtesy.

It may be suggested that the primary school isn't the place to teach manners and they should be taught at home. However, we know that some of our children do not have a home environment that supports the expectations that we might have in school. We cannot take for granted that skills such as turn-taking are something that children have as they enter our nursery and Reception classes. We also cannot assume that these manners will continue to be seen in the same way as the children get older, as getting out of the habit, as well as picking up poorer habits, is easy to fall into.

The simplest thing we can do is to insist on 'please' and 'thank you', something that enters the realms of any classroom at any given day, with the ubiquitous acts of giving out books, taking them back in again and distributing resources. Setting high expectations from the very beginning of every year demonstrates to any child that what they experienced in the previous year will be the consistent and continued expectation in the 12 months to come.

All the adults in the school therefore need to be exceptional role models for manners and they should be rewarding excellent examples as well as picking up on and addressing poor manners.

Suggested learning opportunities and activities for self-awareness

Self-awareness is best promoted through the use of language, but some of our children enter EYFS with little or no language for a range of reasons: language delay, English as an additional language, being non-verbal or family circumstances. Modelling facial expression and body language to show emotions and feelings is important from the very beginning of a child's formal education, particularly if the child arrives at school without this prior experience. Here are some activities to help teach self-awareness explicitly and to support its development in the classroom, followed by a plan for a whole-school assembly based on the theme of resilience.

EYFS	• Use art activities to encourage the children to develop an understanding of facial expression to show different feelings. This could include painting or drawing the facial expression shown by an adult. Children can then be led in discussing the feeling or emotion that a particular face shows. • Introduce the notion of challenge at an early age. Games such as building a marshmallow and spaghetti tower to the greatest height are great fun but also introduce the notion that some tasks are harder than others and that some children will find problems more quickly or may prefer to work alone or in a team. • Introduce positive language into the classroom at the earliest opportunity, with words such as 'kind', 'proud', 'great' and 'thank you'. Embedding these words at this early stage will help in the development of a positive mindset.

KS1	• Build awareness of emotions and feelings through role play. You could perhaps include the use of a puppet hospital, where children communicate with the puppets about feeling and emotion to find out what is wrong with the 'patient'. • Develop resilience through challenges that might form part of a PE lesson, such as aiming and throwing. Alternatively, set challenges relating to sequencing in mathematics and encourage the children to think about why they got stuck and what they did to overcome this challenge.
LKS2	• Encourage the children to think about different mindsets, both fixed and growth. Ask them to think about the impact of asking for help or declining to ask for help. • Model and discuss the kinds of activities that children could take part in to help manage negative emotions. Build these into discussions about choices and ways to manage negative feelings in a positive manner.
UKS2	• Small groups are ideal for allowing children to talk about what self-management means. Children should think about a range of attributes that they might need to demonstrate in a variety of social situations. • Actively teach coping strategies and help children to manage difficult or painful emotions, deal with stressful events and build self-confidence. • Discuss whether different strategies are needed to support different situations. Role-play with the children how they might respond to situations such as being laughed at in class for a particular score in a test or how they might react to an unexpectedly rude friend.

A resilience assembly

Preparation

You will need some origami paper. Alternatively, any other paper cut into squares measuring 20 cm by 20 cm will do the job. Practise some origami beforehand and have some pre-folded and completed work to show at the outset.

You will also need a table at the front of the assembly space to demonstrate the folding in action.

Assembly music

'Paradise' by Coldplay contains lyrics about expectation and keeping going, which suits the theme of this assembly.

Setting the scene

Show some of your prepared origami. Include some simple boats, hats and birds. Choose one that you are going to fold for the children; it should be nothing too complex but challenging enough.

Demonstrate how to fold the design, showing each stage to the audience and keeping up a commentary that will add some drama and tension and draw 'ooh' and 'wow' from the children.

Call up four volunteers, who could include a brave staff member. Tell them to produce what you just have. Don't help or give any instruction. This will inevitably lead to a few mishaps, which is the point of the assembly.

Give the volunteers a further piece of origami paper and this time work alongside them, demonstrating each fold and stopping between each phase of the process. Encourage support from the audience and applause on completion, allowing them to take their finished work back to class.

Reflection

- Ask the children what they have learned from assembly today. Is it just how to fold paper or is it more than this?
- How did the volunteers feel on the first attempt?
- How did the circumstances change on the second occasion?

- Talk about how the volunteers were becoming more resilient by practice, repetition and watching an 'expert' complete a task.
- Invite the audience to suggest situations in which they have got more resilient through these strategies.

Follow-up ideas

- Ask your volunteers to teach other children in their class how to make the same origami.
- Leave out instructions to make different origami, or send them out via homework.
- Invite the children to bring in their work to show in future assemblies.

Success criteria: What does a school that prioritises self-awareness look like?

- The school culture will place a high priority on the value of effective relationships in the classroom, on the playground and in every interaction children have with their peers and adults.
- The school will promote the place of open and honest talk and of the ability of all within the school community to listen.
- Self-awareness will be promoted as part of modelling, scaffolding and teaching of emotional intelligence.
- Children will be able to self-regulate, supported by co-regulation of emotion, which the adults will support.
- Motivation will not be for simple external reward, but for satisfaction of the children's own goals.
- Children can demonstrate that they are empathetic to their classmates, teachers, support staff and parents.
- The school culture will promote good manners and social skills.

3 Healthy lifestyle choices: food and exercise

Chapter overview

This chapter considers the ways in which we can teach and embed healthy eating in our school, thinking beyond the 'healthy plate' to encourage children to make choices for health and lifestyle reasons.

Areas discussed

Learning opportunities and activities

Assembly theme

In primary schools, we do a reasonably good job of delivering lessons on healthy eating within our science curriculum. I would argue, however, that we need to look beyond the 'healthy plate' activity, with the balance of protein and carbohydrates, fats and fibre, vitamins and minerals. The interactive and online programmes that help to plan a model meal or resources that allow for experimentation with variety and colour may go some way to covering the statutory requirements. Nevertheless, we need to go further to show that this is really taught as part of wellbeing, and this demonstrates that our wellbeing curriculum extends beyond the classroom.

School lunches, thanks to the efforts of Jamie Oliver and others, have to provide balance and nutrition alongside portion control. But does our curriculum extend into the children's lunchboxes, or indeed into our school kitchens? We can teach how much vitamin C a pineapple contains, the benefits of chickpeas or the seasonality of satsumas, but if these items never work their way into the dietary habits of our children, we will have delivered the knowledge but not embedded it.

Every lesson on a balanced lunchbox could count for little if packed lunches still include rubbery cheese wrapped in plastic, ham shaped like a teddy bear, or fruit packed into a sticky bar with no small percentage of added sugar. In an ideal world, we would love to see rows of children with healthier choices but the socio-economic circumstances of many of our families, in addition to the food choices their children are able to make, very much restrict the options available to them.

This is where our curriculum comes in – not to suggest that lunchtimes become a science lesson, but to embed some of the principles that our healthy eating lessons could convey with a different mindset. If schools can think beyond the healthy plate, past the lessons that cover the science curriculum alone, we have an opportunity to very much embed healthy eating habits into our children's lifestyles.

The challenges around healthy lifestyles

In my research for this book, many primary teachers expressed concern that parental messages about what constitutes healthy eating were their greatest barrier and challenge to promoting the topic. There are a number of reasons for this, both societal and cultural. What we may consider to be healthy food simply isn't affordable to many of our families; we need to train our staff to be sensitive in addressing this issue with parents, as this is potentially an area where the socio-economic backgrounds of our teaching staff and our families might differ widely. As one respondent to my survey noted:

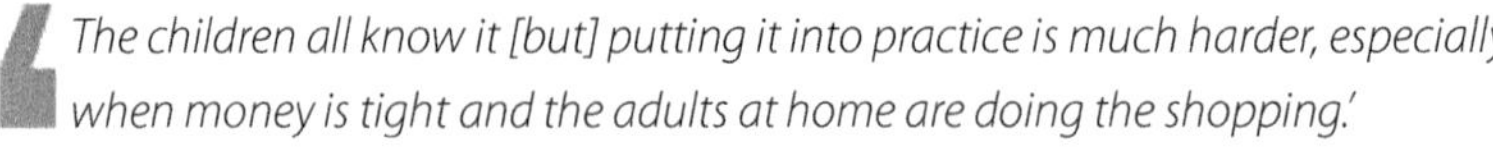

> *The children all know it [but] putting it into practice is much harder, especially when money is tight and the adults at home are doing the shopping.'*

Some teachers also felt that children don't appreciate being 'preached at' in school, but would rather have positive role models to promote an active lifestyle: the teacher who *really* eats a healthy lunch, or the teaching assistant who runs the Daily Mile with the class (see page 41). Other respondents believed that the children lack opportunities in school to develop the theory they have covered.

This again takes us back to covering themes on a set day or week each year but not having further chances to use these skills in a meaningful way.

Embedding healthy food choices in the broader curriculum

In my classrooms, some of the most impactful lessons have come, almost by accident rather than design, through giving the children experience of food and cooking in ways that stretch and challenge constrained views of the curriculum.

In one lesson, to engage a Year 6 class on a wet Friday afternoon in November, the class all brought in a different favourite vegetable and we prepared them in a tempura batter and served them up as they were freshly cooked. Boston beans, cauliflower, carrots and sweet potato were all introduced to the children in a way that gave them ownership of the lesson but with a twist of flavour and adventure. Memorably, one of the boys in the class who had announced his hatred of aubergines 'because they're purple' concluded, 'Actually, they're quite nice.'

Another lesson involved children bringing in their choice of fruit for an art afternoon inspired by Giuseppe Arcimboldo, the Italian artist best known for his portraits made entirely of fruit, vegetables, fish and flowers. The afternoon was spent peeling, chopping and slicing before creating a whole-class portrait, on a four-metre-square plastic table covering. Photographic evidence was captured before the class consumed their artwork. The wider impact of this lesson was in the opportunity to share foods beyond their usual choices. We had a scattering of grapes and strawberries alongside apples and segmented oranges, but for the children who had never before tried watermelon, mango or papaya, starfruit or dragon fruit, this was a new experience. As a school, we were at the time encouraging children to bring healthier snacks for breaktimes. Over the next few weeks, there was a change in snack habits, which rippled through the rest of the school.

Making bread was a lesson that lasted all day and justifiably covered the maths curriculum (measures and ratio) as well as the English curriculum, as we discussed the process, wrote up the instructions and discussed advertisement of our product. Testing the value of patience, as allowing the dough to rise and prove does, the bread the children made, using both wholemeal and white flour in their mixes, was wholesome and enjoyed so much that nothing went home. This enabled the setting of a homework task of working through the recipe at home and bringing samples to school the following week.

With the same class, a morning was spent preparing macaroni cheese, in a lesson which allowed for respect of vegetarianism and veganism, food intolerances and cultural as well as personal preferences. Not only did this lesson provide the class with their lunch that day, but sending the recipe home and allowing the children to organise their family kitchen for an evening had a powerful impact. The feedback I had from parents, along the lines of 'bringing us together as a family' and 'giving our child the chance to lead at home', was beyond anything I had expected.

One class I taught ran an enterprise based around bread. Once they had been taught how to make a loaf, each child made a 50 pence investment. As shareholders they made the decisions about ingredients: white or wholemeal flour, sesame or pumpkin seed toppings. Negotiations were held with the headteacher about use of the staffroom oven and the costs of electricity, whilst other children discussed advertisements and pricing. One group would come to school earlier each morning to prepare the day's batch whilst another dutifully recorded the sales on a spreadsheet. Harsh lessons were learned by the children who didn't let their dough rise sufficiently, sending the profits spiralling on a couple of occasions. At the end of six weeks, though, a healthy profit, more than a twelvefold return on their initial outlay, taught much about a business model.

Healthy eating and exercise within the National Curriculum

The current slimline National Curriculum has some specific references to food and exercise. Year 2 has awareness of the basic human need for food and water and the importance for humans of exercise, eating the right amounts of different types of food, and hygiene. Year 3, meanwhile, mentions nutrition specifically, whilst Year 4 gets onto bones and teeth. By Year 6 children should have been taught about the impact that their nutrition and life choices have upon physical health. There is also non-statutory guidance about looking at the research that supports the relationship between diet, exercise, drugs and lifestyle.

Suggested learning opportunities and activities for food nutrition

Whilst food and nutrition play an obvious part in the National Curriculum, considering the impact of these issues on the children's wellbeing requires an ongoing focus, which will take us at times into the parts of the school day outside the classroom. The lunch hall is part of the school day where manners and social skills, behaviour management and the curriculum come together.

EYFS	• Make food choices available without 'fear', which more often than not comes about from parental perception. The daily fresh fruit and vegetable provision can be quite varied. • Food preparation as part of a weekly routine can cover the importance of food hygiene and introduce the skills of cutting safely, in addition to introducing unfamiliar foods to the children's experience.
KS1	• Introduce the terminology of carbohydrate, protein and fats into discussion. Make the distinction between fat as part of a food group and the use of the term in relation to body shape. Age five to seven is a crucial time to address stereotyping as at this age prejudices can begin to become subconsciously embedded. • Link the food groups to their health benefits: what makes us stronger, helps or harms our teeth, and is useful when we have a cold?
LKS2	• Be specific about nutrients and their identified impact and benefits. • Plan an ideal packed lunch, and use children from this age group as lunch monitors, as they are often sticklers for the rules. Challenging the guidelines for packed lunches often comes from the older children: to be found out by a child in Year 3 is a powerful motivator to comply.
UKS2	• Ask the children to create a healthy eating survey for the adults in school. Checking whether their teacher is eating properly not only reinforces the importance of healthy habits when they see adults following their own guidance, but also promotes a whole-school approach to healthy eating.

	• As part of an enterprise day or week, creating healthy snacks and selling them to children, parents and staff combines economic wellbeing with sharing the ethos of well-balanced and nutritious foods. • Use digital software to track consumption or plan a meal. • Use supermarket shopping websites to track prices and to plan a meal, or a week's shopping, for a family on a specific budget. • Consider what it might be like to make a choice to be vegetarian or vegan. Look at some recipes and try preparing them. Is this a choice the children could make for themselves?

Exercise: a choice beyond PE lessons

Our physical education (PE) lessons offer the opportunity to succeed in competitive sports. Character is specifically referred to in relation to opportunities to compete in sport and to embed the values of fairness and respect. This is contained within the purpose of study and the aims of the PE National Curriculum, the latter of which refer to the leading of healthy and active lives.

Our challenge in school is to ensure that the child who might potentially always be the last pick at team selection, because of the perception others have of their skill and ability, is just as active and engaged in activity as the peer who is always first choice because of their perceived natural ability. Here is also an opportunity to challenge issues of body image so far as they relate to physical activity and ability. Positive reinforcement can be used to challenge the comments and attitudes that some children face from an early age because of weight or disability.

All too often, the image of exercise having to be related to competitive sport has the potential to deter some children. The notion of being 'good' at sport disguises the other options for physical activity, which can be as good, or in many cases better, for lifelong physical health and fitness.

Children should know that some of the benefits of physical activity are that it:

- promotes the growth of new brain cells, improving concentration and memory and hence improving the ability to learn and retain information
- strengthens heart and lungs, increases oxygen intake and promotes muscle growth and repair
- reduces the risk of illness and disease

- reduces the risk of weight gain, high cholesterol and high blood pressure
- strengthens muscles and bones, flexibility and fluidity of joints
- promotes healthy sleep
- positively impacts on mental health through the release of endorphins and dopamine.

Suggested learning opportunities and activities for encouraging physical activity beyond PE lessons

The following activities are suggestions of ways to encourage the children to be involved in physical activity beyond the weekly PE lessons. Reference is made to the Daily Mile, which has become an increasingly popular feature of many schools, run before school begins, at break or at lunchtime. Schools may have a track marked out on the playground and manage this with staggered starts for each class and possibly with adults running with the children as mentors or motivators. Some of the suggestions below require adult guidance, particularly those in EYFS, but as the children grow in confidence, part of their character development will be to take increasing responsibility for their own physical fitness choices.

EYFS	• Racing: any race activity not only promotes muscle development and coordination but also, from the earlier age, the notion of winning graciously and accepting defeat without a feeling of failure. Running, walking, balancing, obstacle racing and using a space hopper all promote sport as a fun activity. • Dance: simple routines build repetition and the making of patterns, yet also develop physical stamina and a range of new movements. • Throwing: to each other, at a target or for distance, throwing activities can use a range of resources that can be adapted for children who are still working on their gross motor control. • Parachutes: every age group, and many adults, love the use of parachute games. Although the children will appreciate the fun element, these games support working safely, teamwork, cooperation and resilience as well as coordination.

KS1	• Make activity part of the daily routine. Online exercise routines with activities that promote movement and do not penalise those who are less coordinated are ideal. • Children can create and design their own 'get moving' ideas and present each one on a card. Once laminated, these can be used as a starter activity or brain break to focus children for the next session, as a warm-up in PE or as an activity for the playground. • Use a body outline to build a picture of which parts of the body are benefiting from exercise. Children can keep their own outlines to record and identify body parts that they need to work on a little more.
LKS2	• Devise a schedule for physical activity during the school day, at home and during weekends and holidays. • Encourage the children to start recording the differences they feel after exercise: heart rate, breathing, temperature and impact on muscles. Can the children evaluate a difference in the way they feel? • From Year 3 onwards, start teaching pacing techniques in the Daily Mile, to sustain a pace without getting out of breath and to avoid the run becoming a walk.
UKS2	• After a sustained period of physical activity, over several weeks, discuss and evaluate the physical and mental differences the children notice: are they physically stronger? Do they concentrate better? Has memory improved? Are they sleeping more soundly? • Devise a programme for younger children to follow at break or in PE involving catching skills, movement, flexibility and changes of direction. • Invent a game with limited resources: a space, a ball and maybe a wall and chalk to define our play zones. Agree the rules. This is especially powerful if the game doesn't involve a winner (king ball comes to mind). • Devise a fitness circuit for a PE lesson or playtime. Devise one for use at home too, thinking about space and resources.

Parental engagement with healthy lifestyles

Engaging parents with your healthy eating aims for the children provides one valuable way to engage them in the values and ethos of the school. If the school is serious in promoting both the physical and mental wellbeing of the children, involving parents has the potential to help them engage more with supporting their children as learners. Many parents will have skills and knowledge in the kitchen that they may be willing to share as visitors to the class, or which they can teach their children at home.

Consider running some parental workshops around healthy packed lunches or on simple family suppers. Rather than launching these out of the blue, build up a series of parent workshops around a general theme of wellbeing and being supportive as a community. Make the sessions around food practical and fun, setting some challenges such as cutting an onion the finest or kneading bread. These sessions are as much about building trust and relationships with the parents as teaching some kitchen skills and recipes.

Never underestimate the impact of involving the whole range of cultures in your school too. I was introduced to jollof rice at my first school, where we had a substantial catchment from the Nigerian community. We hosted an event where we asked families to bring a dish from home, and in addition to the dozen or so variations of this classic dish that we tasted, a range of delicious and homemade dishes were shared across the school community.

Later sessions could include some aspect of exercise. Inviting the parents to work alongside their children in a PE lesson is more likely to succeed in the Early Years, when a greater number of parents might be available during the school day. Equally, bearing in mind the school diary for the year, a session to coincide with sports day, when parents will often be there for the parent race, is an ideal opportunity to capture the attention of an audience.

Once established, these sessions could then include some more impactful information about how a healthy diet affects the children's physical fitness, learning capacity and long-term health.

A healthy living assembly: what is in my food?

The amount of hidden sugar in our food will surprise many of us. Take a close look, for example, at the sugar content of your favourite branded muesli and then compare it to supermarket own brands. Do the same with the microwavable ready meal you may bring for lunch. The high volume of sugar as a preservative and flavour enhancer may make you rethink your weekly shopping choices.

Warning: be aware of the children's context as you plan this assembly. For many children, their parents may have neither the skills nor the time to cook from scratch. Food is a sensitive issue and schools should be wary of being seen to be judgmental about family food choices, particularly if there are a number of families receiving support from the food bank. Foods featured in this assembly should be adapted for and sensitive to your audience.

Preparation

Create a list of prepared slides or cards showing two similar food items to choose from, with the heading: 'Would you rather eat/drink...?' The first option should have a higher sugar content than the second option. Example options could include:

- low-fat flavoured yoghurt or Greek yoghurt
- fruit juice or water
- a jar of pasta sauce or a homemade equivalent
- chocolate milk or plain milk
- frosted cereal or porridge oats.

Prepare some further slides with pictures of foods that children may typically enjoy, but that are very high in sugar content: baked beans, tomato ketchup, iced or filled doughnuts, and fries and burgers from popular fast food chain restaurants. Include the sugar content for each item, perhaps as a percentage.

Choose a few carefully selected children and give them 'planted' answers to stimulate discussion. These answers could be chosen in reference to the sensitivities mentioned above.

Assembly music

'Food Glorious Food' from the musical *Oliver* is a great choice for obvious reasons.

Setting the scene

Ask the adults in the room what they had for their dinner the night before or for breakfast this morning. Build engagement with the children by suitable facial expression and responses, both positive and less enthusiastic.
Ask the same of your 'planted' children: these answers could include some of the ingredients on the slides.

Then ask adults and children alike whether they know what was actually in the food they ate for breakfast. Expect a mix of answers, from the highly detailed to the very simple.

Play the 'would you rather' game using the slides with a show of hands or with a selected panel of children. It is possible, though not guaranteed, that the first option will receive most votes. Whatever the result, take this as the cue to discuss the high sugar content of the first item in each pair.

Follow this by working through the items on the remaining slides, revealing the sugar content for each.

Many of the children should be able to describe some of the consequences of eating too much sugar: tooth decay, weight gain, diabetes. Think about your audience before mentioning heart disease and some cancers as a consequence; leave these out if these diseases have impacted some of your families.

Reflection

- Can we cut out sugar altogether? Explain that moderation is important, that some people will make a choice to have only one sugary treat a day, maybe once a week or sometimes not at all.
- Ask the children how, apart from cutting down our intake, we can protect ourselves against the health impact of sugar. Expect answers relating to brushing of teeth, but also encourage answers that refer to exercise. Create a link here with any exercise programmes that might be ongoing.

Follow-up

- Some classes, perhaps those covering the work in their class at the current time, could conduct a healthy snack survey for the snacks children bring for morning break. This could encourage the bringing of snacks if take-up is low, or could monitor what is being brought in.
- If there is a variety of different food choices in the snacks being brought from home, find a way for the children to explore and promote these so other children can enjoy them too. Mango, papaya, pomegranate and coconut may feature alongside apples, satsumas and bananas.

With statistics for childhood obesity in England showing that 9.7 per cent of Reception-aged children and 20.2 per cent of those in Year 6 were clinically obese in 2018–2019 (NHS Digital, 2019), the place for teaching healthy lifestyles is not only essential but urgent. This latest survey also shows that obesity prevalence is more than double in areas of greater deprivation, and that in Year 6, boys (22.5 per cent) are more likely to be recorded as obese than girls (17.8 per cent), which shows that even though teaching about healthy lifestyles is taking place, in practice a significant number of our children aren't experiencing healthy habits. For the sake of the nation's future health, this aspect of wellbeing needs to be drawn into sharp focus.

Though not covered specifically in the suggested activities in this chapter, teachers should be aware of the issue of body shaming, particularly associated with weight. Of course, it would take quite an insensitive teacher to weigh children in front of the class, or even to use the actual weights of children in a maths or science activity. However, knowing your class, and parents, is essential, particularly as children become more aware of body image through the pressures of social media and name-calling related to size and to diet. The language we use in discussing healthy food options should relate to the health benefits of food first, before considering the negative impacts of imbalance between food groups.

Success criteria: What does a school that prioritises healthy eating and exercise look like?

- Children can identify that their school is committed to healthy lifestyles by looking beyond their physical education and science curricula and by considering the other opportunities that support healthy living.
- Schools will ensure that opportunity is available to everyone, particularly outside of school, allowing as many different children as possible to take part in sporting or physical pursuits in other settings.
- Healthy lunches will be promoted proactively, celebrating the range of positive options available and not sitting in judgement upon less healthy alternatives.
- Parents will be proactively supported in preparing healthier lunches and menus.
- Children will work on their physical resilience by adding a physical activity into their daily routine, and on their nutritional resilience by not showing fears of different or unfamiliar foods.

4 Healthy lifestyle choices: care for the environment

Chapter overview

This chapter will consider the ways in which we can discuss the issue of climate change with our children and raise their interest in wider environmental issues. The focus will be on practical and authentic activities that can enhance the learning, knowledge and experience of our children.

Whilst teachers might think it unlikely that they have the next Greta Thunberg amongst the ranks of their students, we can certainly aspire to help them become eloquent and forthright spokespeople for their environment as they enter and face adulthood and the challenges ahead. It is, after all, the children at primary school today who are going to be the ones who see many technological changes to reduce greenhouse gas emissions become the norm, such as electric cars and solar panels. It is the same children who will face the longer-term impact of the damage that greenhouse gases have caused to our climate and the rise in temperatures causing higher sea levels. Children are also concerned about the effects of deforestation on wildlife and the physical integrity of the landscape. This generation of children need to be equipped with the tools to challenge environmental concerns that impact upon both their physical and economic wellbeing, and to do so in a way that will earn respect and attention, just as Greta Thunberg has modelled so persuasively. If the impacts of genuine character education are going to be felt, through empowering our children to debate and discuss environmental matters in a meaningful and impactful manner, we need to be looking beyond well-meaning phrases and slogans that sound great chanted in assembly but mean little when refuse bins are still packed with plastic bottles and non-recyclable waste products.

Children are so concerned about the environment that a survey from March 2020 conducted by BBC Newsround indicated that some children are losing sleep about environmental issues. Most children interviewed for the survey indicated that they are worried about climate change and one in five suggested they had bad dreams about it. Two in five didn't trust adults to tackle the challenge presented by climate change. Of greater concern was that two thirds of children interviewed didn't believe that leaders were listening enough to their views.

Here then is our justification for teaching children about climate change and helping them to find a way to express their concerns and to raise them in a mature and meaningful manner. Our children may have been influenced by television, particularly by the work of Sir David Attenborough, but they may also be concerned by environmental issues that affect them directly. For example, schools located by particularly busy roads in urban areas may find that their children have a particularly high level of asthma and other breathing difficulties. In my experience, children have raised their concerns with the local authority and community groups in relation to matters as diverse as a local plant being planned to burn waste to produce electricity, and more recently a campaign aimed at supporting the local community where a dump for car tyres caught fire and was belching toxic smoke, which drifted over the school playground with the prevailing wind.

Such local issues provide a starting point for discussion in the classroom and perhaps in the wider school community. Addressing these matters enables children to express how the issue is directly affecting them and how they feel it should be dealt with. This can give the children a sense of ownership of the concern and can also allow them to express their worries directly with the hope of actually getting a positive result. The last thing we would want to see is for our children to make some kind of dramatic gesture, such as chaining themselves to railings. Here lies an opportunity to teach and share the impact of peaceful and reasoned protest, of expressing concerns verbally and in writing with well-thought-through argument, and of involving local and national figures in their campaign.

Raising awareness of the environment in school

'We can all do the easy visual stuff – recycling, reducing single-use plastic, etc. It is harder to respond to the bigger stuff, such as carbon dioxide, when the adults make the decisions.'

The adults make the decisions, as this teacher said in my survey, but we need to consider that our children will be those most affected by current decision-making. Here we will discuss ways of involving children in the serious discussion of air pollution, water shortages, recycling, plastics and biodiversity.

Air

Children in schools located on busy roads, particularly older buildings in our inner cities, will only be too familiar with high levels of pollution linked to road traffic, with evidence sometimes provided by air quality monitoring devices located nearby or on site. Whilst there is little they can do directly to change the amount of toxins in the air, this issue does allow children to practise their negotiation strategies and persuasive skills. Letters to MPs, local councillors and the press, argued in a reasoned manner, will allow the development of essential features of character education.

Where children can make a difference is through parental engagement, with ideal opportunities offered through 'Walk to School' campaigns, such as 'Walk on Wednesday' or 'Walk to School Week'. These campaigns encourage families to notice the sights and sounds of their journey to school and to consider the physical benefits of walking, in addition to the saved cost on petrol and the reduction in harmful emissions.

Water

Children may take the availability of clean water for granted, unless they have realised that water is metered and has to be paid for. Recent hot summers, though, and the impact upon parks and playing fields, may have exposed children to the language of water shortages and what drought conditions may be like. In their science curriculum, the children will find out how the water cycle works, but environmental awareness requires them to know about how water is wasted and what they can do to save water.

Children need to know about water shortages and the effect of drought in countries where rainfall is low and water sources have dried up, leading to food shortages, hygiene and sanitation concerns as well as chronic poverty. They equally need to know that sometimes human intervention may have made this situation worse. If children are taught that in such places water is regarded as a gift or a privilege, they might think twice about leaving a tap running.

By realising that the shortage of water might have such a devastating impact, and that such a volume of water is wasted in this country through dripping taps or fractured pipes, children can be encouraged to consider how much water is used in domestic settings and in their school. If the design of the school allows it, water butts are a simple way of reducing mains water usage. Reusing 'grey' water from handwashing, which would otherwise drain away, whilst environmentally desirable for watering plants, would require a major infrastructure investment.

Reduce, reuse, recycle

The mantra of 'reduce, reuse, recycle' will resonate through many of our schools through inviting the local recycling group in for assembly. However, if the assembly content remains the same year on year, is there not a risk that the message becomes diluted? However well-intentioned it may be, the roll of cardboard taken from individual cereal boxes and the activity of sorting of tins, bottles and newspapers into the correct bins does become familiar, as the children will only too freely let their teachers know.

'Reduce, reuse, recycle' needs to be more than an assembly; it needs to be a daily occurrence and should be promoted as part of the school and classroom routine – in other words, it needs to be 'lived' rather than be an annual event. A clear message that reduction of paper wastage is a school priority can come from adults in the school reusing backing for display or using hessian fabric or 'rescued' wallpaper rather than expensive backing paper. Whilst this may be regarded as a gesture, it clearly states the intention of the school. Persuasive adult guidance, from something as simple as sharing worksheets, repurposing unused sides of misfed photocopying paper and ensuring that every scrap and trimming ends up in the recycling bin, embeds a message that the school wishes to be green. Primary school teachers are by their nature resourceful, and thinking beyond junk modelling to giving an item a genuine second life can enable a mindset around reuse to develop. Nowhere is this more apparent than with the issue of plastic.

Plastic

Here is where the current generation of children can make a sizeable and perceptible difference. David Attenborough's campaign, so eloquently expressed in *Blue Planet II*, clearly communicated the issues around plastic. Point out to children that every single piece of plastic ever produced still exists somewhere and the impact becomes more sobering. Introduce the term 'micro-plastics' into their vocabulary. Tell the children that these have been found in the guts of fish, sharks and other sea creatures, and this brings plastics into the human food chain. The potential effect on health and physical wellbeing needs to be understood. Take a local walk to witness the impact of plastic littering and carelessness by adults, and the children can see the evidence for themselves. In my experience, my classes have seen fishing lines wrapped around ducks' feet, plastic rings that are used to hold together multipacks of canned drinks trapping swans by their necks, and the natural beauty of a local river spoiled by irresponsible dumping upstream. Children shouldn't be exposed to this for shock value, but to create enough of a moral stance for them to take it further.

If you have an active stance on plastics, the children will soon enthusiastically join in. Having taken the children on a local environmental walk, they can be encouraged to go out with their families to see this for themselves. I have known several families, especially in the 2020 lockdown, take an active role in litter-picking and cleaning out ponds and stream beds, often on the initiative and urging of their children. On a domestic level, reduction of plastic usage in the home can be driven by the example set in school. Teachers drinking from reusable and sustainable water bottles, rather than the single-use bottles sold commercially, sets an example. Some schools may choose to ban single-use plastics from their sites altogether. This may be a challenge, particularly with pre-packed drinks in lunch boxes, but it is an area where environmental leaders can work with the healthy eating monitors to support a wider aspect of school wellbeing and character strategy.

Schools interested in developing their newer teachers or members of their support staff may consider appointing one to lead their recycling strategy. This could involve leading assemblies, organising on-site litter-picking and making care of the environment part of the ongoing agenda in schools. If the message comes from school leadership alone, it risks being lost, but if it is led by an adult the children see every day, it can add impetus to pupil engagement. Taking responsibility for an annual or once-a-term focused event, particularly one involving the community, can add impetus if it is different and stands out. My school drew positive attention to the issue of plastics one Christmas. Invited to prepare a tree for the local church, rather than take a real one, we constructed our Christmas tree from plastic bottles with decorations made from recycled materials. Contrasting with the real trees from other schools, it certainly gave a clear message to the community about our intentions in regard to plastics and the environment.

Biodiversity

When the children are interested in recycling and reducing plastic usage, the school's biodiversity strategy could be extended to ensure that plants, animals and ecosystems on site are conserved, protected and enhanced, and that there is a measure of tracking this over time. This is an ideal task for your potential environmental leaders (see Chapter 10, page 152).

Learning about and enjoying the wildlife of the school and the immediate locality makes an important contribution to the children's quality of life, health and spiritual wellbeing. School grounds provide an excellent site for children to learn about biodiversity. Children need to know that plants, animals and habitats enrich our everyday lives, as they produce the necessary ingredients for all life to exist. Without conserving biodiversity, we will pass to our successors a planet that is markedly poorer than the one we were privileged to inherit. By teaching that we all have a duty of care to the environment, we promote its protection for generations to come, and by increasing biodiversity in school, we can raise environmental awareness in our local communities.

Improving school grounds can influence children's values and attitudes towards the wider environment. Whilst the size and location of primary schools may limit the potential for promoting a biodiverse environment, there are a few simple steps that can be taken to maintain a level of interest in protecting nature in the school locality:

- Build a pond. If there isn't room on site, typical of many inner-city schools, a repurposed water tank, an old-fashioned sink or a half barrel could be converted into a pond. Be wary of health and safety regulations.
- Plant native species of trees, shrubs and hedgerows. These will help to attract a wide range of insects, birds and small mammals that feed on them. Schools without green space can use suitably sized pots, which can be watered using the rainfall collected in the water butts.
- Bird boxes, protected from rainfall and direct sunshine, will provide safe spaces for breeding and allow the children to see fledglings close up.
- Setting up bird feeders (perhaps built as part of a recycling and reusing project), bee and bug 'hotels' and 'wild corners', and keeping old logs and leaves as potential homes for insects and hedgehogs are simple projects the children can take responsibility for.

Biodiversity does not stop at the school fence. Many local authorities have a local environmental centre, which has a cost implication but which gives a larger-scale model of care for the environment than the school could provide. There is green space within walking distance of almost every school, a free resource that maybe we don't use as often as we could but, being within our community, it is one we should encourage the children to appreciate and respect.

Conservation

Children may not be familiar with statistics relating to the destruction of the Amazonian rainforest. Even expressing how many trees are being destroyed each week in terms of numbers of football pitches, though a dramatic figure, is hard to imagine for children for whom the concept of area is difficult. In considering conservation, and in particular deforestation, though it is important to know about what is happening to rainforests and why trees are being cut down, looking closer to home may be a better starting point.

In many urban locations, there is often pressure to build on open spaces; parks, playing fields and allotments all typically appear in local news stories alongside pictures of protestors. The children might be surprised that these unlikely eco-warriors aren't the kind who dig tunnels or chain themselves to diggers, as seen on the national news on a high-profile campaign, but are more likely to be a dog walker, jogger or local volunteer. Seeing someone they might know protesting peacefully but eloquently and persistently can illustrate to the children the value of the natural resources in their locality and the effect that a well-coordinated campaign can have.

Gardening in the curriculum

There is no simpler way of helping children to contribute to a healthy environment than encouraging them to grow their own green space. To do so in school can add beauty to what might otherwise be an uninspiring structure, but may also motivate the children to take their enthusiasm and new-found knowledge home and to build garden spaces with their families and in the wider community.

The wellbeing and character opportunities offered by gardening are immense and could be highly effective. With a little imagination, planning and foresight, the horticultural experience that we provide in our primary schools enables life opportunities that support care for the environment, promote healthy living and inspire an interest that can cross generations. It also offers a chance for the children to grow, and then cook, their own food.

Gardening for wellbeing

The simple act of being outside is, in itself, supportive of our mental health; the addition of an activity, be it digging, hoeing, watering or harvesting, is a way of keeping physically fit, which may suit those less inclined to sports pursuits. Garden journalists are already referring to a 'green revolution' and few outside activities can achieve as much for the mind and the soul as horticulture can. Revelling in and contemplating nature, its colours, aromas, rewards and challenges supports mental and physical wellbeing. Gardening is also a sociable pastime, promoting social interaction, even at a social distance.

The national lockdown through the spring and early summer of 2020 saw an upsurge in interest for gardening amongst children. More time with family, together with near-perfect growing conditions, allowed children the opportunity to experiment with flowers, fruit and vegetables and to share the images with their schools. Fans of the BBC's *Gardeners' World* will be more than familiar with the video clips sent in through the summer, many of which were sent in by children proud of their projects and produce. The impetus to develop this youthful zest and energy for all things horticultural is there to be built upon.

Gardening and character

This aspect of the children's environmental education entirely suits our agenda for character education in a number of ways. Firstly, it represents a way of demonstrating pride in the school and a sense of belonging. A well-maintained patch, even out of growing season, shows an element of care for the school and the wider environment, and provides a point of conversation and discussion that children could have with visitors. This is also a powerful motivator for behaviour too. Try this with a child who demonstrates challenges in the classroom. The natural flow of discussion in the garden will provide a different focal point and engage a sense of pride and achievement as well as ownership.

Resilience and patience are likewise supported through work in the garden. The value of patience can be established through the simple fact that the growth of vegetables takes so long. Planning and preparation, thinking ahead to the end product and being prepared to recognise that nature sometimes doesn't take the course we might have intended – all are lessons in life skills that could not be delivered in the classroom.

As part of a strong co-curriculum, horticulture is an ideal partner. It enables the direct teaching of terms such as organic and mulch, of seasonality and of companion planting. It can also promote a sense of pride in the school in terms of the appearance of the gardening area, whether in full bloom or in the part of the garden cycle where flowers fade but the space still has structure. The cyclical nature of gardening teaches children the value of preparation and not to depend on the instant gratification that completing a test or a task in a limited time often results in.

Volunteering is well served through gardening. Where time and human resources permit, try taking a group into the community to support elderly people, perhaps in developing a sensory garden in a local care home, or dressing out a hanging basket or trough for a nearby resident. If the school has an allotment, growing crops for the local community offers the opportunity to run a small-scale enterprise or to support families through a food bank.

Equality of opportunity can be addressed through gardening, which is a great leveller. Children who find spelling, arithmetic or PE a challenge will soon realise that 'progress' in gardening is so very different from the classroom. Being focused on practical skills and promoting the values of perseverance, resilience and patience, 'success' in gardening takes time and is judged not on test scores. Neither does 'success' need to rely upon the height of sunflowers or the weight of vegetables, but on less quantifiable and more aesthetic factors, such as protecting the crop from pests and diseases, being innovative in watering, and the physical presentation of the garden space.

'I don't have the space to garden'

In my previous school, we were fortunate enough to have a dedicated garden space within our forest school environment. We had space for a greenhouse and several raised beds, and several young apple trees, planted to celebrate the name of the school: Orchard. Schools with less or no green space may ask how they might teach gardening, but a little imagination and creativity can allow even the smallest area of tarmac or paving to become a tiny garden paradise. Here are some ideas to get you started:

- Classrooms with outside access can have hanging baskets attached along the walls. These baskets are ideal for flowers but also tumbling varieties of tomatoes or strawberries, and in the space below, any arrangement of pots, dependent on the dimensions of the space, can be added.

- Avoid the purchase of expensive raised planters by applying the mantra of 'reuse and recycle'. To promote the reuse of plastics, try using empty compost bags or empty five-litre PVA glue or paint containers. Two-litre bottles with the tops removed can be used individually or joined into a 'honeycomb' with a few dabs of PVA (the primary teacher's best friend, as it lasts forever) to provide a long root run.
- Use of a range of items that might otherwise be disposed of can also allow the promotion of the 'reuse and recycle' message, although do ensure that they are cleaned, sharp edges are removed and holes for drainage are drilled. Old paint cans, stacks of car tyres, wooden crates from the local greengrocer or even an old chest of drawers make interesting and varied containers. Worn-out wellington boots can also serve as containers, with vegetation bursting forth from the top or holes cut into the toes.
- If there is the facility nearby, consider the hire of an allotment that is relatively cheap and can be divided easily to give each class an area to work upon. A regular weekly or fortnightly visit can easily be timetabled.
- One of the most effective uses of a playing field I have seen was to allocate an area of the field for vegetable plots for each class. The arrangement of the plots in rows, each with a marker post showing the class teacher's name, had the unfortunate, though amusing, effect of looking like a teachers' cemetery. Come the end of the summer term, the wealth of flowers and vegetables was a welcoming return on the investment of time.

Gardening within the National Curriculum

Gardening clearly fits within the curriculum for science, from naming plants and trees in Year 1 to identifying seasonal change in Year 2. In Key Stage 1, the germination of seed and conditions to grow are covered, and as the children reach Key Stage 2, the life cycle of plants is covered. Thinking more widely, the mathematics curriculum allows for a wealth of opportunities for measurement and recording of data, design technology allows for building structures in the garden, and the teaching of history can include how people in the past learned from the patterns of nature and grew according to the seasons and the prevailing conditions. The study of plants that originate elsewhere in the world is an ideal way to discuss the impact of other cultures on our habits – the potato, for example!

Suggested learning opportunities and activities for environmental topics and gardening

These activities, supporting environmental topics and the development of the school garden, are intended to be progressive, building upon each other so that children become aware of the challenges that their environment faces, as well as building a sense of love of gardening and respect for the environment.

EYFS	• This is the point when the teaching of tidiness and cleaning up after ourselves can be modelled and become habitual. Everyone being responsible for one space and the introduction of monitors is one way into showing the children they are trusted and can look after the spaces around them. • Go on a litter 'scavenger hunt', particularly if the boundary fences of the school are next to public footpaths. Engage EYFS parents in a clean-up; put a positive spin on this activity by celebrating those who make the effort to respect the environment, rather than giving a negative account of those who litter. • Use your indoor space, such as window ledges, to teach the children about germination. Something that sprouts within days can hook the children for life. Use outdoor spaces to teach patience and resilience with vegetables; potatoes and tomatoes started after the spring half term can be ready in time for the summer. • Teach about conditions for growth of plants by sowing seed in contrasting locations: bright or shaded; damp or dry; warm or cool; in different composts or soils; and in different containers. The early exposure to finding the correct conditions can also teach that success in gardening is not always guaranteed and needs a measure of skill as well as of luck to work. • Take the children on a sensory walk around the school site. Encourage them to take their time, to touch, to smell and to listen. Whether you have a forest school space or are on a site with little greenery, knowing and appreciating what is there can connect the children to their space and enforce their pride in their surroundings.

KS1	• Write an open letter to the local community about littering on and around the school site. Local councillors, press and voluntary groups will often take this seriously and draw attention to the matter. This will show children that sharing concerns can have an impact. • Include recycling and reusing projects as part of the art and design curriculum; bird boxes and feeders and bug hotels show that such activities aren't tokens but have an actual value. • In gardening, introduce herbs into the planting programme to promote companion planting (basil with tomatoes, for example) as well as seasonality; thyme is quite hardy whereas basil is tender and needs warm temperatures. • Plan and plant a wildflower space. This could be temporary – in a pot or raised bed – or more permanent if space permits. It will encourage bees and other pollinators, enriching other aspects of the curriculum.
LKS2	• As a voluntary project, organise a litter-pick off site. A local path or park would be ideal for this. The amount of plastic and other items that could be recycled will be highlighted, as will the impact on the environment and community if there is visible damage. This needs a careful risk assessment, as some local parks may be littered with drug paraphernalia, beer cans and broken bottles. • Investigate the different conditions where germination and growth are successful or hindered. Plan these into planting cycles as the children move into older year groups.
UKS2	• Proactively teach that so many consumer items, typically clothing, are 'throwaway'. Take recycling and reusing to a different plane by introducing upcycling. Promote economic wellbeing by reusing clothing, whether taking a plain t-shirt and customising it, or taking outgrown jeans and other items and repurposing them for a younger wearer. Ambitious teachers may do the same with household or school furniture items that might otherwise be disposed of. • Plan a sensory garden for the school or for a community group. Investigate suitable plants, being aware of allergies and selecting plants for texture and scent.

An environmental assembly

This is an interactive assembly that can be very effective in teaching the children the impact of flushing the wrong materials down the sink and down the toilet. Appealing to the odd fascination for gunk and goo that many children have, this presentation allows children to think about how to deal with fatbergs.

Preparation

Ahead of the assembly, prepare two two-litre bottles filled with tap water and have to hand some toilet tissue and some baby wipes. For your PowerPoint presentation, make sure you have pictures of some fatbergs, preferably with a human standing by them for a sense of scale.

Assembly music

Choose any song that celebrates the simple pleasures of our environment, for example, 'Morning Has Broken' by Cat Stevens or 'It's a Wonderful World' by Louis Armstrong.

Setting the scene

Ask the children what kinds of things they flushed down the sink this morning. Expect answers such as toothpaste and water.

Ask what kinds of things the adults may have tipped down the sink. If they don't say otherwise, ask whether it is appropriate to pour cooking oil or food items down the sink.

Then ask what kinds of things *should* be flushed down the toilet. Expect a few giggles at this point! Trust the children to say what should be flushed down the toilet but then ask what other things might be involved. You may be quite surprised by the responses; when I've done this assembly, I've had responses as diverse as cooking fat, dead animals and homework. This will allow a transition to the practical part of the assembly.

Invite two children to the front. In one bottle, place the toilet tissue; in the other, the wet wipe. Give each child one of the bottles. On your word, they shake their bottle as vigorously as they can for around 20 seconds. The toilet tissue will disintegrate, just as it does in real life. The wet wipe will stubbornly remain intact. Explain that, when the wet wipe is flushed down the toilet, it will travel down the pipe like this and get stuck in the drains either on the property or out in the street.

Repeat the same experiment with dark-coloured cooking oil and water. However much the children shake the bottle, the oil will always coalesce together and remain separate. If flushed down the toilet or thrown down the sink, oil will solidify and cause a blockage in the drains. Reveal the images of fatbergs on your PowerPoint slides to show the scale of the problem.

Reflection

Ask the children to consider what can be safely disposed of down the bathroom/kitchen sink or the toilet and why this should be happening. Take the view that this is safe, hygienic and responsible.

Follow-up

In class, create a fatberg to demonstrate just how easily one forms. Wipes, cooking oil, clean food waste and some leaf debris would be a start. Allow it to safely chill in a fridge (or outside on a cold day). Use of a length of pipe or a tall and narrow measuring jug will teach children how difficult these are to remove.

Encourage the children to monitor what goes down the drain at home. This could encourage the use of bathroom bins to deposit wipes, kitchen caddies for the collection of food waste or creating reminders about using the correct bins for each type of waste. This can be followed up in class or at a subsequent assembly.

Success criteria: What does a school that prioritises the environment look like?

- When we teach about the environment, children take pride in what they do for their surroundings, respect what they have in their community and are eloquent in speaking up against what they see as wrong.
- Children know what 'reduce, reuse, recycle' means and it isn't simply a catchphrase.
- Our daily activities encourage respect for the environment. Scrap paper goes to a tray for reuse. We teach about using the recycling bin and placing the correct items in it.
- Children actively show they want to reduce plastic usage and save water.
- Children can express their concerns about air quality, traffic pollution, littering, conservation and biodiversity in their locality. They can eloquently take their worries for the national or global picture and share these with people of influence.
- Children show a love for growing food and flowers and appreciate the economic, environmental and aesthetic results they bring.
- A love for the environment extends into children's activities in the home and in the local community.

5 Healthy lifestyle choices: personal safety

Chapter overview

To conclude the section on 'Knowing ourselves', this chapter addresses issues of personal safety, a long-standing staple of the school year, often delivered by outside providers who are perhaps more expert in their field than teachers. As with much of the other content of this book, the concepts are often seen as a one-off event each year but, given their importance, need to be part of a continual pastoral and educational conversation with the children.

Believe the words of certain influential speakers on education, and the 1950s is seen as some kind of idyllic age; post-war, post-rationing, it is touted as an age of relative innocence before the sexual and societal revolution of the 1960s. It was apparently a safer place too, where children could play outside and where the threat of gangs, drugs and bad language was a lifetime away. Of course, it wasn't necessarily a safer time, but it was very different from today in the ways in which concerns for personal safety manifested themselves. The risks on the road have been present since the invention of the car, looking out for strangers has been a mantra of parents for decades, and the anti-social presence of gangs was an issue in the '50s and '60s; however, all of these dangers have changed in terms of the level of risk associated with them.

This chapter isn't about danger, but about safety and helping children make the decisions that are going to keep them safe through their time at primary school and equip them with the skills to avoid risk as they move on to secondary.

Road safety

Road safety is one of those aspects of PSHE that, on the surface, is a little fusty and dated. Road safety campaigns of the past are of their time, such as the Green Cross Code, made famous by the late Dave Prowse (latterly Darth Vader) as the Green Cross Man. Nevertheless, the current 'Think!' campaign does cover some excellent core material, which can provide a sound basis for learning about road safety in a meaningful manner.

Consider road safety within the broader context of personal safety, and we have a meatier proposition on our hands, because ultimately the EYFS experience of playing at crossing patrols needs to build into an awareness of risk avoidance as our children become increasingly independent. For the youngest children, they would need an idea of what traffic is and about the weight, size and speed of it; this is a challenging concept to explain, but one that small world play and stories would explain very well. Depending upon the school location, some kind of survey or observation of traffic should probably form part of the curriculum regularly through the children's school life, not as a paper exercise but as a meaningful activity to show the volume of traffic around a school. Consistently conducted surveys can also show a pattern of traffic over time, a persuasive resource for Key Stage 2 pupils seeking to be junior citizens.

In 2019, the number of fatalities on British roads was the lowest it had been for years. What these statistics don't show, though, are the numbers of near misses – the times drivers have been forced to break suddenly or when a child has been pulled back from the roadside by a peer or a parent.

The following are possible risks near to the school, which lessons and assemblies should address pre-emptively, rather than the danger being outlined in a parental newsletter when it may by then be too late:

- Children distracted by a mobile phone: whether calling parents or listening to music, are they 100 per cent attentive to the road?

- Children gathered in a group on the roadside: a little 'horsing around' could easily result in one or more children stepping into the road or distracting passing drivers.
- Children leaving school by micro-scooter: these can pick up quite a speed and can be a hazard on the road or pavement.
- Young children not being closely supervised by parents: the risk speaks for itself here.
- Parents running late at either end of the day.

The volume of traffic on roads, particularly in urban areas, and roads near schools packed with parked cars add to the potential hazards facing pedestrians and drivers. In my experience, from schools in a 'new town' environment, where children crossed roads by underpasses or bridges, to those on a side road, where the traffic is greatly increased at drop-off and pick-up times, the greater road risk to our children is always on the roads nearest to the school and from vehicles driven by someone in the school community.

Road safety needs to be a habit modelled by adults and poor practice needs to be highlighted and discussed too. Collectively, we must have lost count of the numbers of adults we have seen crossing the road just metres from a crossing, unaware of traffic because of the distraction of headphones or engaged in animated conversation with little awareness of the road. Helping children to identify safe places and safe ways to cross roads will not only help keep them safe but also enable them to speak up to adults about being safe, which has been a focus of recent public information campaigns such as 'Watch your speed; your child does', a powerful reminder to parents. Indeed, our road safety work should also focus upon behaviour in a vehicle and avoiding distraction for the driver as well as other road users.

Suggested learning opportunities and activities for road safety

EYFS	• Use the outside role play area, as well as small world play, to model the language of safety in addition to safe behaviours. Children in role as a crossing patrol, deciding when it is safe to cross, have an ideal opportunity to develop their vocabulary related to this core aspect of their safety. • Any kind of sorting activity into 'safe' and 'unsafe', such as with places to cross or being with an adult, also develops the language of being safe and alert.

KS1	• Introduce the notion of crossing unfamiliar roads. School trips are ideal for this, particularly when crossing busy roads. • Use the local traffic surveys to write letters to alert parents to local risk factors on the roads near the school; pupil voice, as opposed to teacher voice, will have greater impact.
LKS2	• 'Hands up' surveys are quite revealing in this part of the school, particularly regarding attitudes to risk. Children are becoming more independent and might dare to run across the road or take a chance. It's interesting to share these findings with parents. • Run some specific lessons about being able to judge speed as a roadside observer; the children will soon realise that this is very difficult to judge because of their relative inexperience of the road. They also need to realise that their visibility to drivers is impacted by the colour or brightness of their clothing.
UKS2	• Your Junior Road Safety Officers are crucial here (see page 153). At this point, road safety might not be regarded as especially 'cool' but it is essential. Children in Years 5 and 6 are typically going to be trusted to make their own way to school, and with a reduction in road crossing patrols, the risk is heightened. • In maths lessons, look at stopping distances in dry and wet conditions. This has long been part of the Highway Code. Marking these in chalk on the playground will provide a strong visual reminder of how long it takes a fast-moving vehicle to come to a stop. • Use input from the local transport authority to embed safe conduct whilst travelling on public transport: standing back from the kerb, not standing on the stairs or on the top deck of the bus, and respecting the rules around ticketing and transport passes. This is a crucial part of the transition to secondary school and demonstrates the strength of the children's good character.

'Stranger danger': who keeps us safe?

We used to teach something called 'stranger danger' in an age pre-internet, before interactive games and smartphones. The 'strangers' also fitted a stereotype: they hung around by parks and schools, wore dirty raincoats, had an unsavoury smell, offered sweets and puppies, and were invariably male. The initiative may well have led to a climate of fear and suspicion.

It took cases like the Soham murders, where the school caretaker was convicted, and the Little Ted's Nursery in Devon, leading to the conviction of a female member of staff for the abuse of toddlers, for some people to realise that the threats aren't always from strangers but can be from people the children know and trust. Safeguarding has promoted greater awareness amongst teachers of the people likely to offer threats to our children, and that if children are harmed the perpetrator is more likely to be someone they know, but this shouldn't disguise the fact that strangers still need to be treated carefully. Any opportunity to address and challenge stereotyping should be taken here, as in many other aspects of character education.

Again, the focus should be on safety rather than on danger – facts, not fear – but reality tells us that, though most people are trustworthy, we cannot tell whether they are or not, and we should never simply trust someone because they have a badge or hold a position of authority. As adults, we know this; for children, there is a fine line between creating a culture of distrusting everyone they don't know and one where they have a healthy scepticism. This is difficult to teach.

To explain 'stranger danger' to children, calmly explain a stranger is somebody the class or the family doesn't know. Explain that, whilst it is acceptable and polite for them to talk to someone new if an adult is with them, it isn't safe for them to talk to unknown adults on their own. Model that, if the child is alone and an adult approaches them, they should treat the adult as a stranger. This needs to be more nuanced than 'Don't talk to strangers', as it can, as the children become more mature, include an awareness of their 'gut instinct', which develops as they learn more about trust.

Teaching children to walk away, to come back to school, to shout aloud for help or to find other trusted adults, such as a police officer, if worried about someone are actions that parents might teach at home, but are essential topics to cover at school as well. So too is teaching about guarding against sharing personal information, just as we would teach with regard to e-safety; personalised backpacks and football shirts with names added mean a child's name is there for all to see.

The most important theme of personal welfare has to relate to how the children respond if they are worried for their safety. Much of this goes back to their early language development and how they are taught to address different matters that arise in their lives. Teaching children how to speak to different audiences, to be aware of themselves and who they are speaking to, is essential; whilst it is not unknown for a child to announce something significant aloud to the rest of the class, they are more likely to say something to a teacher or teaching assistant. This will be particularly the case with incidents of domestic abuse or children being left hungry overnight. Chapter 9 on trust will develop this theme further.

Suggested learning opportunities and activities for keeping safe from strangers

Though the onus for personal safety should lie with the parents, our commitment to the children through safeguarding means we need to be keeping this subject on the agenda, as children will encounter adults new to them on school visits, residential trips and in their lives outside of school. Activities should always include an element of what to do if concerned, whom and how to tell, alongside how to keep safe.

EYFS	• Place the emphasis on being safe: with whom should we go outside? (Parents, relatives, teachers and teaching assistants.) • Who else keeps us safe? A perennial Early Years topic, there is still plenty of scope for teaching about firefighters, police officers and medical staff, and plentiful opportunities to show respect for diversity too. • Role play and storytelling play an important part here too, particularly using traditional tales.
KS1	• Introduce the notion of what a stranger is but avoid the word 'danger'. Point out instead that a stranger is someone we don't know and who looks just like anyone else. • Role-play situations such as what to do if children get lost. Some will have had this experience already in moments when their own attention or that of their parents was momentarily diverted. Reinforce the concept of a 'safer stranger', which might include shop staff in addition to those referred to above. The idea of a safer building – a shop, a police station or another school – is worth introducing here too. • Let the children know that they should never go somewhere on their own with someone they don't know.

LKS2	• Think about language. Adults may ask children questions and, though it may be innocent, sometimes it isn't. Role-play how to answer questions around school and home, friends and family, with a firm but polite response. 'Sorry, but I don't know you!' is a simple and effective strategy, as is the advice to 'Yell, run, tell!', though this may need some modelling to avoid road risks. • Use your lessons to reinforce the idea of stereotyping. We don't necessarily need to reference stereotyping a stranger, because this strategy works just as effectively with any kind of stereotyping.
UKS2	• Encourage the children at this age, when they may be travelling to and from school without an adult, to agree a 'charter' for safe travel to be shared with parents. It could include always travelling with a friend, agreeing a safe route, walking along the pavements of main roads and linking to how to cross roads safely. • Make links also with your e-safety lessons. Would we accept an invitation from a person we meet on the street or online?

Coughs and sneezes spread diseases

This section was only ever intended to be a short and passing look at an aspect of health education often covered within the modelling of good manners. Events since the beginning of 2020 make the importance of this topic only too obvious for wellbeing education. We often tell newly qualified teachers that they will build their immunity in the first few years, but what might have seemed a mildly amusing anecdote about seasonal colds and skin infections should be treated more seriously than this, as any teacher who has been infected by chickenpox or measles (potentially with serious health implications for adults) will attest.

Hand hygiene

The coronavirus pandemic has seen a greater emphasis on handwashing than ever before, with a quick shake of the hands under a tap and a wipe of the hands down a jumper, which the most vigilant midday staff notice from some distance, being addressed from necessity. As schools, we have rightly placed an emphasis on this in the Early Years, but school systems, the pressures of time and possibly the assumption that, once the children know how, they will continue in the same vein mean this may not have been enforced. We should not be reinforcing and reteaching this because of the pandemic; it should be in place as a life habit.

Reminder posters, temporary sanitising stations and references to singing *Happy Birthday* through twice disguise the fact that many primary school toilet facilities aren't terribly nice places to be because of the smell, the state of the facilities and because it is a place where adults cannot monitor behaviour. The blocking of plugholes and the drawing of pictures in soap on the mirrors can distract children from the importance of hygiene. There is no simple solution, because the location and extent of facilities are so different in each school. Good management of the washrooms in our school buildings is something unique to each institution, but something we need to be proactive about to support our young learners.

Respiratory hygiene

Airborne transmission is responsible for the round of colds and coughs that are a feature of our school year, and whilst again some people might argue there is a case for parents to teach this, the reality of school tells us that runny noses and uncovered coughs are routine. Again, healthy habits need to be embedded and engaged, recognised and rewarded. This doesn't require a sticker for using a tissue, but a simple 'well done and thank you for covering your mouth when you coughed', which acknowledges the action, draws positive attention and alerts others to how they might earn similar praise.

The availability of tissues is essential. Though some schools might insist children bring their own, we need to put good health first; children and parents do forget such essentials and may have financial and other circumstances to consider.

Food hygiene

Teaching effectively about the importance of food hygiene has a twofold impact. Firstly, teachers can address the importance of cleanliness before, during and after school or when eating packed lunches. Dropped sandwiches picked off the floor, taking fries from the plate of a classmate and inadvertently sharing glasses of water are regular occurrences that don't require a rebuke but a quiet reminder to stop them becoming an unhealthy habit. This fits within the wider picture of good manners at lunchtime, which can be led by dedicated midday supervision and which will address use of cutlery and lunch trays as well as appropriate food disposal.

Secondly, and more closely linked to the National Curriculum, is the cleanliness in food preparation. Schools fortunate enough to have a lunchtime provider who will provide lessons on food preparation are at an advantage, but lest we forget, there is a part of the design technology curriculum that concerns food. Whether your school is fortunate enough to have a dedicated area for cooking lessons to take place or not, simple routines of cleanliness around handwashing, preparation of surfaces, handling and cutting food can be put into place from the Early Years and become a habit in as much as we would embed good social interaction and behaviour expectations.

Suggested learning opportunities and activities for personal hygiene

EYFS	• The daily routine, one of the core parts of planning in EYFS, is the place to have the habits of good health hygiene taught and made part of good conduct and manners. Though many of our children will arrive with these habits established, others may not, so the place of modelling healthy habits and how it benefits everyone are only too clear. • The importance of thorough handwashing can be demonstrated through the 'sprinkles' activity. Place damp hands into a bowl of cake sprinkles or glitter. The challenge for the children is to wash off the sprinkles, which represent germs. They will realise that they need to wash between the fingers, under the nails and over the backs of the hands to remove evidence of infection. • Use the plentiful opportunities to work with food at snack times, on special occasions like birthdays and celebrations, and when children cut, spread, grate and mash raw or cooked foods to make the hygiene side of the food preparation routine evident.

KS1	• Remind the children of how much they touch in the course of a few minutes: their faces, each other, tables, books, pencils. Go on to mention how often their fingers are in their mouths. The notion of the hands as a germ farm may sound a little extreme, but it is one way that some infections, such as the norovirus, can rip through a classroom with some velocity. • Invent some interactive games with a focus on personal hygiene: do the children consider the washing of clothes as essential as the brushing of teeth? • Arrange a visit to the school kitchen, with a specific brief to consider the different arrangements. Where are utensils stored? How are trays and cutlery cleaned? Why are there four colours of chopping boards? How are the fridges organised?
LKS2	• By this age, children may start becoming more sensitive to personal hygiene issues, particularly if they notice this in one of their peers. In my experience, children complaining about head lice, body odour and other related matters can lead to embarrassment, possible bullying and disruption to learning. As part of class behaviour routines, establish ways of being sensitive to others' needs and in how we speak to and about each other. • Give children of this age responsibility for the school campaign about hygiene; they are old enough to be listened to by younger children and this gives them a taste of responsibility. The posters about washing and drying hands, disposing of tissues and other healthy habits have added weight with the voice of pupils rather than adults. • Linking to the RE curriculum, consider how food is handled in different faiths, in particular during key festivals. To be able to understand belief-based aspects of food during festivals such as Ramadan, Pessach or Lent will promote the children's respect for diversity, add to their understanding of different cultures and show the universality of encouraging healthy ways of eating.

UKS2	• By Year 5, habits should be embedded. Rather than a pack drill of instructions about handwashing, contextualising the impact of disease on society shows the children it is nothing new and hygiene is an essential feature of good character in society. • History lessons are an ideal time to teach some knowledge about the history of disease and infection control, particularly if this is your school's chosen theme through a period of time. Of especial pertinence would be to look at outbreaks of bubonic plague, which London schools cover alongside the Great Fire. Of further interest is the story of the village of Eyam, an early example of social distancing to prevent spread of infection. • Victorian history allows a look at the public works designed to address cholera and typhoid. Whilst the topic is of interest in itself, the link to wellbeing is how easy it was for now preventable disease to spread. This is also an ideal opportunity to teach the value of public service. • In food technology lessons, work through complete recipes that can be shared at home. Choose bread, macaroni cheese or vegan and vegetarian dishes that allow opportunity to use food technology skills yet also have an end product that will give meaning to the hygiene aspect of the activity.

Alcohol, drugs and tobacco

This aspect of the PSHE curriculum is a regular and reliable part of teaching, fitting within the boundaries of primary science. Again, like the other aspects of personal safety, it is possible that more emphasis may be placed on danger rather than safe conduct. The stark realities, however, are that children will be only too familiar with the language, terminology and impact of alcohol, drugs and tobacco in the lives of their families and communities.

Is it possible, though, that we are painting these as 'dirty' words. For example, do we only think of alcohol in terms of alcoholism and the draining impact it has on vulnerable families? Should we consider talking about it as something that can be socially acceptable when treated responsibly? After all, when we consider teaching the history of Victorian England, weak ale was actually preferred to the drinking of water, as what was provided through the taps and pumps was actually a source of typhoid and cholera. Likewise, with the term 'drugs', are we thinking only of the behaviour of those addicted to illegal substances? Do we not consider that medication such as inhalers, steroids or even something as innocent as junior doses of liquid paracetamol are also deemed drugs, simply because they are taken by choice to have an impact upon the body?

Many of us will have had the experience of the children saying, 'There's a bag of weed on the playground' or heard the use of words like 'skunk', 'skag' and 'grass' in the classroom. Whilst there is a potential safeguarding issue with this, which should never be ignored, we should also acknowledge that children know more than we sometimes recognise. Simply because they know this language, does it mean they are exposed to a risk, or does it mean they recognise the risk?

Similarly with alcohol, which takes up several aisles of many supermarkets, do we approach it as an evil, or as a choice? Whilst certain nations, faiths and aspects of society do not embrace the consumption of alcohol, which we should respect and discuss as appropriate, the fact that alcohol is often gifted to teachers at Christmas and at the end of the year should encourage all of us to recognise there are aspects of self-regulation that we should discuss with children.

Tobacco, though hidden from view since the laws about advertisement and sales have changed, still plays a part in the family lives of many children. As an addictive substance, tobacco has a comparable impact upon economic wellbeing as much as secondary or passive smoking has on physical wellbeing. Although the physical harms of smoking will be taught in school, the social (or anti-social) side of tobacco consumption needs to be considered too. Secondary colleagues tell me that smoking is still seen as a status symbol, of being tough or intimidating, or as a part of gang culture, either as a sign of membership or of initiation.

Any discussion of drugs regretfully has to contain reference to the phenomenon of county lines, a drain and an invasive influence on the lives of many of our teenage children. Whilst there is little evidence so far of primary-aged children being involved in county lines, the potential vulnerabilities of children likely to be dragged into such abhorrent activity need to be recognised far more in our primary school classrooms. The lines in this case are the phone lines, referring to the cheap but untraceable mobile phones gifted to young carriers. The lines may also reference the railway lines that run out of our major cities into rural and small-town environments. Whilst I would not advocate teaching about county lines to primary school children, coverage of peer pressure and gangs is certainly something to consider, particularly as a transition package for Year 6 to Year 7.

Here the safe bubble of primary school suddenly becomes a more worrisome environment and children with lower self-esteem or those who appear to be streetwise might be vulnerable to being drawn into the circle of those wishing to exploit their naivety.

Suggested learning opportunities and activities for alcohol, drugs and tobacco

EYFS	• Right from the start of school, lessons should be about making healthy choices, as they would be with any other aspect of personal safety. Introduce the vocabulary of medication, such as ointment, tablets or injection into role play, as Reception or nursery is likely to have a surgery or hospital in their role play area at some point of the school year. This is the time to start teaching that medicines are given for a reason and that they are for the patient only. • Model the safe handling of medicines. Placing inhalers and other medication on a high shelf is a clear indication to the children of this, as well as an obvious safety point.
KS1	• As the children get older, more specific reference to safe handling of household substances can be made alongside teaching about medicine. As the children learn how the body works, they can make links to how medicines help to cure and to prevent disease.
LKS2	• Start to introduce the risks and effects of drugs, alcohol and tobacco. At this age, the specific detail covered may depend upon the social experience of the children, particularly if there is addiction in the family. Knowing your families is important, and a more sensitive choice of language might be more appropriate here. • Build or purchase a 'smoking machine', which demonstrates very clearly what happens as smoke is drawn into the lungs.

UKS2	• Ask the children to draw 'a bag of drugs' that they might have seen by the side of the road. This can be revealing of the children's prior knowledge and experience. As a teacher, you can complete this activity too, and ask any additional adults to do likewise. Children may draw tobacco and alcohol if taught well lower in the school. The revealing part will be if they are able to name any illegal drugs, which could reflect their exposure to the media or to life in the local area. Always be aware of safeguarding concerns arising from the children's answers. As an adult, your 'bag' can include tea and coffee, headache tablets, an inhaler and so on, to emphasise that 'drugs' aren't always the illegal variety. • Teach specifically the management of pressure and influences, including those from peers and what the children may read online or see on the television. • Teach children how they can seek help and support for themselves or others in relation to health and substances, particularly in Year 6 transition.

An assembly on keeping safe

Preparation

Gather the following resources before the assembly:

- a builder's hard hat from the EYFS role play box
- one egg (with a face drawn onto it) and a clear plastic bowl, or a plastic tablecloth
- traffic cones from the PE cupboard or road safety role play equipment
- barriers that are placed around a hole in the road (many schools have these now as part of equipment to separate bubbles)
- a 'danger' sign.

Prepare a PowerPoint presentation showing images of a range of potential domestic dangers: a hot saucepan with the handle turned outwards, a hot radiator, a frayed electrical flex, an open baby gate, and scissors and kitchen knives left unattended. The slides should also include images of outdoor situations that could be unsafe with careless actions: a flooded quarry, rivers and streams, building sites and busy roads (make these local and relevant to your school).

Assembly music

'Hole in the Ground' by Bernard Cribbins will go with the initial visual representation of this assembly. 'Safe from Harm' by Massive Attack goes with the overarching theme.

Setting the scene

Draw the children's attention to the word 'danger' on the sign. Read the word together as a whole school and remind the children it means that there could be danger if we don't act safely.

Choose a child to wear the hard hat, tapping it to show how hard it is. Explain that its role is to protect the brain, which is the body's computer. Go on to say that sometimes people take risks and decide not to wear their hard hat.

Give the egg a suitably funny name like Eggward. Explain that he is one of those characters who thinks he knows best and that rules don't apply to him, and today he won't wear his hard hat. Let the child in the hard hat drop the egg into the bowl or onto the tablecloth. What does this tell us? Direct your questioning so the children conclude that Eggward wasn't acting safely.

Now ask the child in the hard hat and a group of selected children to place the cones, barriers and danger sign around an imaginary hole so that a potential danger is made as safe as possible. Ask the audience whether there is anything they can do to make it safer.

Work through the domestic slides. Why do parents warn us about these dangers? What do they want you to understand? Use your questioning to direct answers to the natural inquisitive response of children and not knowing what risk is. How do our adults make these situations safe for us?

Now work through the local outdoor slides. By using local issues and particularly drawing on parental concerns, we can highlight ways of being safe. Having taught in a school a matter of metres from the River Thames, such assemblies always referred to tides, mudflats and quicksand, hidden hazards under murky water, not to walk there alone and certainly not to swim.

Reflection

Ask the children what this assembly was actually about. Was it about danger or was it about keeping safe? Take a vote. How strong the majority is towards safety is the evaluation of your assembly. Remind the children that stopping, then thinking before doing anything, is the best way to keep safe.

Follow-up

- Individual classes might wish to use this assembly as a starting point for the other aspects of personal safety, which are sometimes better covered in an age-appropriate manner rather than on a whole-school level.
- Create a 'keeping safe' display in a prominent place. The children can take responsibility for organising the work that is displayed. A mix of art, writing, photographs and captions will draw the eye to it. As with every good display, ensure that it isn't mere decoration but a useful, interactive and regularly updated part of the school.
- Encourage the school council to promote safe conduct as part of its role. Going on part of the health and safety walk with the appointed governor, identifying trip hazards such as chairs or resources not stored properly, or monitoring student movement through the building on the way to assembly or break, are some ways to promote a culture of safety, rather than one of danger.

Success criteria: What does a school that prioritises personal safety look like?

- Personal safety is a regular feature of the school year. It isn't dry and dusty, and the content is so familiar that children could recite your assembly for you.
- The teaching of personal safety aims to showcase the school in the community and encourages children to look out for themselves, their peers, families and others. It allows children to demonstrate how behavioural expectations are set out and embodied in the school culture and it shows, through active participation, that everyone in the school is valued.
- Children independently demonstrate safe attitudes to the road and to traffic.
- They have strategies to keep themselves safe when away from known adults and if they find themselves lost.
- Standards of personal hygiene across the school demonstrate high expectations and an awareness of the needs of others.
- Children are aware of the risks of drugs, alcohol and tobacco and what to do if they have a concern.
- Your emphasis as a school, and the children's perception of this, is on keeping safe, not just avoiding danger. Language counts.

PART 2

Knowing others

6 Looking after others

Chapter overview

Section 2 of this book, 'Knowing others', opens with a consideration of how we expect children to look after others, and to look out for others, themes that ripple through the remainder of the book.

Children are, in the main, naturally sociable creatures. The bonds they forge in their first days of school last, as many a tearful Year 6 leaving assembly will attest to. When they first gather, in nursery or Reception, the skill and kindness of the teaching staff bring those children together in the sand tray, role play corner or mud kitchen, and the way the children play, talk and laugh helps them to form the relationships that will take them through the rest of their primary school days. Do we teach them what a friend is and what friendship looks like? Do we encourage compassion and help them to mend friendships and deal with the child who says they haven't got any friends?

I raise this question because many of us will have seen how some children new to school, particularly in Year 2 and above, slip seamlessly into a class, whilst others can sometimes remain on the margins and not fit within the perceived social structure of the class group. Early Years teachers are excellent practitioners in addressing social skills with children in their first days of school. This is why it is so important to identify all those children with speech, language and communication difficulties, and crucially those who need support in their emotional development. As children extend and elaborate their creative and constructive play, they can begin to show respect for and inclusion of newcomers to a group. Establishments that have clear boundaries and routines can help children to develop appropriate ways to talk and to resolve conflict. In schools where this can develop consistently, the children have a firm foundation in the social and academic interactions for the years ahead, especially if they are able to build respectful relationships with their peers. It is essential that children have plentiful opportunities to work with children outside of their friendship group so that they can build the most effective social skills. Where this is not established, children who arrive new to the school in later years may face social marginalisation, or be inappropriately assertive in trying to break into friendship groups. By contrast, a new arrival with excellent communication and interpersonal skills, the stereotypical 'popular' child, could upset the existing social order.

Bullying

Children think about looking after each other and, particularly when they consider the times when children can be unkind to each other, the language naturally turns to that of bullying. When does behaviour become bullying? Many others will have dealt with, or in the future will face, situations that have been described as bullying. Schools need to be very clear in what their definition of bullying is. One individual incident, although unpleasant, isn't bullying in itself. However, if this is repeated then it might be bullying.

In researching this book, teachers responded that what worked well were stories and role play but also having a very consistent approach through the whole school day. It is vital that midday staff apply the same principles and actions as the staff in the classroom. The most useful practice that many found was summarised by one respondent as follows:

> *'A clear definition of bullying helps. Children need to understand the difference between falling out with friends and bullying.'*

An anti-bullying charter

In my last school, as part of a review of behaviour, we looked at bullying and took pupil voice as a starting point. Starting in Early Years and working my way through the school, I spoke to each class in turn, asking what made the school a safe and happy place and what kinds of things worried them. At no point did I mention the word 'bullying' until the children did so, which they did in Year 1. We then sought to define bullying in the children's terms. Each class agreed to every point, including the younger classes' thoughts, with a democratic vote. Every decision is theirs, and the charter that was created is signed by every child and member of staff at the beginning of the new school year.

This charter is reproduced below. Rather than copy it for your own document, please be prepared to sound out your children's voices, so your charter fits your context.

Anti-bullying charter
We believe everyone at our school has the right to be safe, secure and happy. We asked every child in the school what they thought bullying was and what they can do to stop it if it happens. The best way is to tell.
Who do we tell? A teacher A teaching assistant A midday supervisor The headteacher The deputy headteacher The family liaison officer A friend A family member
What do we tell? What happened Who was involved When it happened
How do we tell? Quietly Discreetly Seriously Write it down Ask for 'two minutes of your time'

Here is what the children agreed:
Reception agreed to make the school a happy place: • We would keep the school clean and tidy. • Children should be nice and play with their friends. • If children argue, they should tell the teacher. • Children should say sorry if they are rude, naughty or do something wrong. • Children should not be rude, throw things or hurt others.
Year 1 agreed: • With what Reception said. • Bullying is when something happens more than once and keeps happening. • We should help someone who is crying. **Year 1 agreed these things could be bullying:** • Saying rude things and using rude words • Laughing at people • Pushing • Pinching • Punching • Kicking
Year 2 agreed: • With what Reception and Year 1 said. • Everyone should be treated the same. • If we see someone on their own, we should look after them. **Year 2 agreed these things could be bullying:** • Using a rude voice • Spoiling someone's game • Tripping someone up • Blaming other children for things

Year 3 agreed:

- With what Reception, Year 1 and Year 2 said.

Year 3 agreed these things could be bullying:

- Damaging property
- Poking with a stick
- Teasing
- Rubbishing someone
- Name calling
- Swearing
- Whispering about someone
- Ignoring someone
- Ganging up
- Threatening language or behaviour
- Spreading rumours

Year 4 agreed:

- With what Reception, Year 1, Year 2 and Year 3 said.

Year 4 agreed these things could be bullying:

- Breaking promises
- Excluding someone from a group or a game
- Calling someone a 'snitch' or a 'grass'
- Saying nasty things about someone's family
- Forcing someone to do something
- Mocking
- Giving dirty looks

Year 5 agreed:

- With what Reception, Year 1, Year 2, Year 3 and Year 4 said.

Year 5 agreed these things could be bullying:

- Racist language
- Sexist language
- Joining in with bad behaviour or poor language
- Stealing
- Cyberbullying

Year 6 agreed:

- With what Reception, Year 1, Year 2, Year 3, Year 4 and Year 5 said.

Year 6 agreed these things could be bullying:

- Saying mean things
- Passing notes
- Taking your own problems out on others
- Making someone jealous
- Drawing attention to differences
- Being mean to a new person – judging them on appearance without knowing them
- Discriminating against disability
- Making someone feel like an outcast or 'invisible'
- Giving mean nicknames
- Frightening or scaring someone
- Using homophobic language
- Judging someone by their choice of friends
- Comments drawing attention to weight or height, accents, hair style or fashion sense
- Laughing at somebody's mistakes
- Being critical of the religion of other children

The charter grows as the children move through the school, so the Year 6 class has the complete piece on their wall. It is discussed anew at the beginning of each year and signed by all in the class community, including teachers and teaching assistants.

Reasons why children bully others

If a child has been involved in bullying, never ask them why in the first instance, because the response will likely blame the victim, list excuses or most commonly be met by a shrug of the shoulders and a resigned 'dunno', which gets us nowhere. We will find out the reasons why, and sometimes this might lead into other areas of investigation, such as a need as yet unrecognised or possibly an issue related to home life that intervention, possibly related to safeguarding, could address.

We should also be extremely careful of stereotyping a bully and also stereotyping their behaviours. Consider these bullies from popular culture, both wonderfully written: Draco Malfoy, Harry Potter's nemesis, and Gripper Stebson from *Grange Hill*, who relentlessly pursued Roland Browning before embarking on racist bullying. With both characters, we only encounter them when involved in bullying, and when found out in a position of weakness. However, bullying is much more nuanced, and oafish and loud behaviour is not typical conduct; bullying with words, and especially cyberbullying (see Chapter 8), dispels many of the archetypal images of the school bully. Many children who have good social skills are also able to turn such behaviours on and off like a tap.

There are a number of common reasons given as to why children become involved in bullying behaviours. These include:

- feeling powerless
- low self-esteem
- winning admiration from others
- fear of missing out or not being part of a group
- lack of empathy for those bullied
- expression of anger
- a culture of bullying and aggression at home, in the community or possibly at school
- being bullied themselves.

We should also be wary of stereotyping children because of those circumstances. Not all children who witness domestic violence become bullies, nor do all those with low self-esteem go on to turn on other children. Likewise, a child who has taken part in bullying actions is still part of the class community and we need to recognise that they have the potential to change and learn from their mistakes.

Can we teach kindness?

An oft-used, overused and misused hashtag on social media in early 2020 was #BeKind. In primary schools, we are used to initiatives such as random acts of kindness, kindness days, weeks or months. But what is kindness? What does kindness mean to a four-year-old and how does it look when they reach 11?

Kindness, as a human value, needs to be modelled and exemplified. It doesn't require reward, need recognition or demand attention. Sometimes it can go unacknowledged, though this does not mean it is unnoticed or lacks value. In teaching kindness, we need to model how it becomes a habit rather than a choice; some children, and adults, will need to think carefully about their actions and the consequences of them. We also need to give consideration to how genuine the kindness that we see is. For adults, many acts of kindness they receive can lack depth or meaning. They could be perceived as a mere token or as intended to draw attention more to the giver than the person in receipt of the act.

This presents us with an opportunity to address the teaching of kindness by addressing the inauthentic manner in which it can appear; there is no better time to do so than in the years in which we can make empathetic kindness a habit. There are three broad categories of fake kindness: performative, manipulative and 'over-sweetened'.

Performative kindness can also be defined as insincerity. In short, it is for show. Adults might typically broadcast this in a social media post, such as 'Just seen your message, I'm here for you': out there for the world to see. This isn't kindness at all but a well-intended but clumsy attempt to express care and concern for someone, because it isn't meant and isn't followed up. In school, this may translate to a child announcing, for the adults to hear, that they are 'looking after' someone after a fall or an incident. This could be genuine, but equally could be part of a game of being top of the class or playground hierarchy.

Kindness can also be manipulative; in other words, there is something to gain from being kind. As adults, we are acutely aware when this happens to us, as it can feel quite uncomfortable. We may have witnessed the person turning on the charm at the airport check-in to worm their way into an upgrade. For our young charges, the child sitting bolt upright with finger on lips to show they are ready to go to break first may also be the child who talked during the lesson or didn't get much down on their page. As adults, we can become distrustful of authentic interactions; as teachers, we hope we can tell the difference.

Over-sweetened kindness is the sort that is suffocating: being shown just how much we are liked, how much that person cares, giving a complimentary or positive response to everything said or done. Though it may be done with the best of intentions, and is genuine in wanting to make others feel good, it can be oppressive; sometimes we just want to be ourselves and need time to ourselves. This form of kindness understands that the object of kindness should be other people, but misunderstands the goal of authentic kindness. It's not to make people feel positive all the time; kindness is there to make people feel validated, seen and respected.

Telling a child to 'be kind' will mean little to them without the experience of what genuine kindness looks like. If the experience of the child is one of the above examples, from a tender age there is a risk that kind acts are for a disingenuous reason, rather than something that should be natural and honest. Hooking a child into habits we define as acts of kindness is something our EYFS colleagues are expert in modelling and encouraging. From small world play to the sand tray, in exploring forest school and in the ways our youngest children begin to work together, there lie a multitude of opportunities to allow children to work together and to help each other. EYFS staff are well versed in noticing small details; I would urge any teacher in any phase to spend half a day in Reception to witness this. This is where kindness can be identified but also shared. The quietest children may seemingly pass under the radar, but it is the quiet ones who often show the empathetic qualities we would wish to see in everyone. Recognition of this, in whole-class time, draws positive attention to a positive act: 'I noticed Samira helping Billy when he was finding it hard to put the bricks together. That was a kind thing to do. Thank you!' A simple act, one with no motive other than wanting to help, is so easily recognised and more impactful than a request to be kind.

Embedded into the school culture at an early age, authentic kindness that is honestly and openly recognised is a way to scaffold such behaviour for those children who might find this more of a challenge, and for those who only feel that they are noticed when they do something wrong, not for doing something right. Recognition need not necessarily be in the form of a reward, but the act of thanks validates the child's actions and choices and marks another positive interaction in the course of a busy school day.

Choosing kindness and taking part in events such as World Kindness Day every 13 November or in random acts of kindness, examples of which are listed in any number of 'Kindness Calendars' (often designed for Advent), can further demonstrate to the children the commitment the school has to the care of children, staff and parents. A powerful text for teaching kindness with the older children is *Wonder* by R. J. Palacio (2012). Set in school, it is a book where the protagonist is a boy with a craniofacial difference, but at its heart it is about kindness. The class teacher writes, 'If you have a choice between being right and being kind, choose kind', a quote from the late Dr Wayne W. Dyer, as a theme for the school year. It is an excellent motivational quote, but we should be teaching that choosing kind is the right thing to do.

Cate Knight is an experienced teacher, both in the UK and internationally. She describes herself as a 'kindness advocate' and has been instrumental in the #KeepingItKind hashtag on Twitter. I am delighted to share Cate's thoughts here.

A study in kindness, by Cate Knight

For those of us who recognise kindness, it may seem that it isn't necessary to explicitly teach it. Surely that happens at home, right? Unfortunately, not always. The teens who struggle with interactions in secondary school are a combination of acquired childhood experiences. If modelled and taught kindness are absent in childhood then they may continue to be absent in the young person right through to adulthood.

Imagine a world that was more kind. If every young learner became consciously aware of kindness, what it involves and what it looks like, then society would look (and feel) very different. We are facing a rising tide of mental health problems in our learners, and our resources are stretched thin. It is time to start educating not just for grades and exam prowess. We need to educate for kindness, empathy, compassion and cohesion.

In teaching kindness, we can help young learners to make autonomous choices around the subjects of morality, ethics and right and wrong. We can help them to understand what makes people happy, how to cultivate this and how to practise self-kindness: the greatest kindness of all.

Kindness is not to be confused with 'niceness'. It requires authenticity and honesty. It can mean making hard choices that don't seem 'nice' at the time but ultimately will help the most people. Kindness is about being able to separate from conformity and make independent choices. It allows our young learners to embrace their uniqueness through a positive lens.

In a world where pressure is in abundance and technology can separate us as much as it connects, it is time to teach something that will never lose its value or meaning in life.

It's time to start keeping it kind.

Teaching forgiveness

Margaret Mizen MBE is a remarkable woman. Within hours of the shocking death of her son Jimmy in May 2008, Margaret had said that she didn't feel anger, as anger breeds anger and that was what had killed her son and could destroy her family too. Margaret and her husband Barry, also awarded an MBE, continue to speak out about what happened to try to bring something good out of tragedy. When Margaret and her son Danny visit schools in the work they now do for the Mizen Foundation, they talk about what happened to Jimmy. There is no escaping the reality of what happened that day, but they emphasise the importance of having a safe space that children can go to if they are worried that something will happen to them. Margaret and I spoke at length about the work of the Mizen Foundation and her hopes and fears for the future.

An interview with Margaret Mizen

Can we teach forgiveness as such?

Forgiveness in itself is difficult for young children to understand, and teachers I have met often worry because children don't forgive. It is more important to teach children about not being angry. Especially when children are approaching transition to secondary school, the level of self-confidence they have in dealing with new challenges they face is crucial. Life in school should not just be about education and qualifications; it should be about life skills.

What are your current concerns based on your work in schools?

Knife crime has increased markedly in the early part of 2021. I believe that children do not think of the consequences of their actions. Bullying is rife, of both children and adults, and the bullying is physical and verbal. In schools there is the pressure on staff and then the children to have good results, but this should not be the be all and end all. The pressure the children are under is taking lives and this frightens me. I speak in prisons and talk to young people convicted of knife crime, though we are not a knife crime charity. They cry at what they have done and at the circumstances they find themselves in.

What can we do about this?

We have to show our children love. They need to know how much they matter and how much they are loved, including the 'naughty' ones. This is nobody's fault; it is the nature of society, the time families have to sit down and talk together, and the pressures of social media. We need to let children feel special, and we need to take them for their worth. We should never give up and we need to make each of them feel valued. There should be a sparkle around kindness, so that their whole being sparkles. [The 'Sparkle Award', awarded to young people for being kind, caring and helpful, is in its planning stage at the time of writing.]

What message would you like the readers to take away with them?

I would like them to think about the Safe Havens, which we talk about in our school visits. Safe Havens are shops and local businesses where children can turn to if they feel they are in danger. They are about rebuilding communities and taking young children beyond the school gates to build bonds with their local community, shopkeepers, police, members of parliament, faith leaders and parents. If I had to sum up our message in three words they would be forgiveness, peace and hope. Our children need to be valued and loved. Our children just need to be children.

Looking after others in the National Curriculum

Aside from the opportunity to develop spoken language, there is little in the pages of the National Curriculum about looking after each other. However, like in much of this book, it doesn't take much of a stretch of the imagination to include it in our stories and role play examples and ensure care for others forms part of the language and experience of the lesson. Stories with a strong moral purpose, some of which are listed in the Further reading section, provide excellent starting points.

Suggested learning opportunities and activities for looking after others

EYFS	• Use every opportunity to praise kindness where it is seen, not for reward but as a positive trait. • Make friendship cards and give friendship rewards so that, from the outset, friendship is valued. • Take every opportunity to celebrate sharing, caring and good manners to embed the language and behaviour of kindness wherever possible.
KS1	• Hold a discussion about what friends do and what friends are. How did you make friends with another person in school? Do you have friends outside of school? How valuable is a friend? • Teach the children the three parts of a genuine apology. Firstly, the act of saying sorry, then an acknowledgement of what has been done wrong and finally what is going to be done to ensure it doesn't happen again. Continue to reinforce this as a model as the children continue to grow through the school. • Proactively mix up your class groupings, especially in foundation subjects including PE, so that the culture of working with each other is embedded early and can be continued through the school.

LKS2	• Have regular discussions about bullying to reinforce that bullying is a continued and deliberate series of actions, not one incident of wrongdoing. • Model how children can challenge bullying behaviour, as a witness or as a victim of bullying, and emphasise the importance of letting an adult in school know as soon as possible. • Appoint children as 'kindness detectives' who can identify acts of kindness in class and from other year groups on the playground, so small acts of kindness can be recognised. Encourage the children to recognise kindness in adults too.
UKS2	• Hold a debate about what compassion means and what it looks like to children at different ages. Consider the impact of a lack of compassion. • Discuss how and why people forgive and how people make amends. Sharing stories, such as the Coventry Blitz and the apologies made by the Luftwaffe pilot who felt guilty at the destruction his bombs caused, shows that forgiveness is part of understanding and empathy.

A kindness assembly

I am grateful again to Cate Knight for drawing my attention to the 17 Sustainable Development Goals adopted by the United Nations and intended to be achieved in 2030 (see https://sdgs.un.org/goals). I adapted several of these into the weekly 'kindness assemblies' I delivered in my own school, each of which set a task for the children to complete.

Goal number 2 aims to achieve zero hunger, with the UN estimating nine per cent of the world's population going to bed hungry each night. The following assembly takes this as its theme.

Preparation

Bring in a number of food items and attach a tag to each one to show its price. Prepare a presentation with pictures of children who are clearly hungry and statistics relating to hunger around the world.

Please be sensitive to your audience here. There may be families who struggle to put food on the table. If so, adapting one of the other Sustainable Development Goals might be more appropriate for the context of your school.

Assembly music

'Willow' by Joan Armatrading. The message of this song is about someone who stands by their friend through everything, epitomising kindness.

Setting the scene

Begin the assembly by asking the children to look at the pictures on the PowerPoint slides without discussion. Give them 20–30 seconds to take in each image before asking for their thoughts and feelings about what they see.

Establish that the children in these pictures are not only hungry but starving. Introduce terms such as 'malnutrition' and 'the poverty line' to the children in the audience.

Explain that many people in the world have to survive on less than £1 a day. The true figure is less than this but the £1 figure will give a stark image to the children.

Reflection

Look now at the food items; which could your £1 afford? Which are essential or luxury? Which of you could survive on £1 a day? Remind children this is the reality for a number of children.

Follow-up

Choose a number of volunteers and set them the following task.

> *You and your family have £1 each to prepare a meal. You can combine your money to purchase items for one meal. You have one week to look up prices and prepare the menu for this meal based on the limits of the money you have. Bring this back to next week's assembly to share your findings.*

When I ran this assembly in my school, the children who completed this task either looked at the prices of online shopping or jotted down the prices on their next family shopping trip. One child took the task to its literal extension and her family actually prepared a meal with the £5 allocated. Returning to the assembly the following week, these children were able to share with the rest of the school just how challenging the task was. Coinciding with the week of Harvest Festival, we gave context to our contributions to the local food bank.

Success criteria: What does a school that prioritises looking after others look like?

- Children understand what friendship means, how friends are made and what friendship is worth.
- Children can identify what bullying is and are able to challenge it by telling adults and by the responses they make. Children also try to avoid being engaged in such behaviour.
- Kindness is valued, for intrinsic recognition and because it is a reflection of universal values of good behaviour.
- Children are able to give an apology and say it like it is meant and valued.
- In the school there is a spirit of forgiveness as part of a lesson in learning from our mistakes.

7 E-safety

Chapter overview

This chapter will discuss the value and the risks associated with digital wellbeing and how the children interact with information online, within the school environment and, crucially, beyond it. We will discuss how to address current concerns about e-safety and how to engage children effectively without striking fear or temptation into them. There is a postscript to this chapter, considering the impact on e-safety through lockdown learning and the reality of digital overload on our school community.

Many schools enjoy Safer Internet Day each February, and the UK Safer Internet Centre produces excellent and appropriate material to support the day in schools. In focusing the attention of schools and parents on something that is integral to the lives of our young people, Safer Internet Day allows for a whole-school focus at one particular time. However, as a school community, we have of course become increasingly dependent upon access to the internet in our daily lives. This is highlighted through the experience of lockdown and the need to have children learning online in the effort to keep them engaged in their learning. We have seen the delivery of online learning through platforms offered by individual schools and by means of lessons from providers such as BBC Teach and Oak National Academy. At a time when some parents are trying to wean children off 'digital dependency', striking the balance from an educational perspective is a challenge.

From sounding out parental concerns about digital usage during lockdown, many schools found that there was recognition that switching from the teaching platform to a game or video was no more than a click away. Parents also expressed their fears of the darker side of the internet and how to protect their children from this unknown and potentially sinister side of on-screen activity.

Nonetheless, we do not need to scare the children away from the internet. It is after all an essential tool in our teaching and the children's learning and one with which we engage several times in the course of a day, from checking the speed recall of times tables to investigating the truth behind a fact or opinion. Embracing the value of digital life permits and enables the children to explore their world and at the same time to discover that not everything they read is necessarily true. Before we consider embracing and celebrating the benefits that life online can bring, we first need to weigh up the challenges that our digital dependency brings.

The challenges of the online world

> *'Our challenge is the constant new tech and social media sources that children are exposed to. Often adults are the last to know when there is an issue. We need a young, switched-on, savvy IT person who can share potential new issues with staff.'*

This teacher succinctly stated in my survey the issue the adults face in teaching e-safety in class, but the challenges the children face online are markedly different from our own childhood experiences. The following section summarises some of the pressures children find themselves facing in their digital lives.

Popular culture

A culture shift of the twenty-first century has been towards an increasing dependence upon devices, social media, online forums and spaces where users interact with others, both the familiar and the unknown. Many adults seem to spend much of their day on email, gaming or social media; just look on the train, by the pool on holiday, in restaurants and bars. It has become an obsession and a perceived need and, whilst we might seek to justify it in terms of communication and keeping in touch, or even for helping our wellbeing (we can after all have mindfulness and relaxation apps on our smartphones), we are, as adults, in danger of becoming controlled by our online existence.

For children, this shift has also been in their access to popular culture. Formerly driven through the power of television, more experienced colleagues will have been used to playtime games based around the *Teenage Mutant Ninja Turtles* or *Mighty Morphin Power Rangers* and the play fighting turning into a little more rough and tumble. Trends spread by word of mouth: does anybody care to remember 'Pogs' or the recurrent themes of yo-yos or loom bands? These days, though, Donatello Turtle or the Green Power Ranger are replaced by characters, themes and trends from online games such as Fortnite or Minecraft.

Whereas playground conduct can be impacted by what the children are seeing in their own environment, it is the ways in which they access online content that impact upon their wellbeing and character development. Consider the experience of parents' evening, when a lively toddler might be handed a parent's phone to distract their attention whilst the appointment is held, or children playing a game online as they wait for the school gate to open. From the age of two, children are not only familiar with but also becoming reliant upon devices for entertainment; for their adults, the phone has become a means to calm, control and coerce. We are in an age where digital life is a part of popular culture, but one where, without firm boundaries, it could dominate the lives and thoughts of the current generation of primary-aged children.

Device envy

There was a time when the brand of trainer a child wore could, quite unfairly, determine their place in the class hierarchy, much in the same way that the sportswear brand they dressed in on non-uniform days might be used as a means of social exclusion or bullying. Brands became a status symbol, resulting in some schools making the wearing of a logo a breach of the uniform policy. For a while, schools were dealing with theft of trainers and tracksuits, sometimes forcibly removed from the owner by a group or gang.

Fast-forward to a time when children have access to or ownership of smartphones and we have a situation where the phone, or devices the children have at home, becomes an object to boast about, or might be used to shame. Many teachers, particularly of Year 6 classes, will be familiar with the chatter about who has which generation of iPhone or other device and will have seen for themselves the embarrassment some children feel at not having the same devices as others. The same can apply equally to other devices at home: brands of tablets, laptops or gaming devices. Where children are more *au fait* or familiar with such consoles, the language becomes almost alien to us as professionals. We will have heard the children's conversations about which device they are getting for Christmas, birthdays or doing well in their work. We will also be familiar with the line from a child, or sometimes from a parent, that they *need* the phone.

The danger here for the children is that their language and their interest relate purely to the device and what it is capable of doing, rather than the safety elements of its use. Dramatic though it may sound, give a ten-year-old child unsupervised access to a smartphone and they are literally one misguided click away from pornographers, stalkers, hackers and those with even darker thoughts on their minds. Yet our children have in their hands a device that allows such access almost unfettered without clear boundaries being set.

Whether a phone, tablet or gaming console, each has a boasting value as much as a financial one. The risk of theft, either in school or if children take their devices out of their bags or pockets on the way home, is not one that school leaders would like to gamble with, nor is the risk of children calling or messaging on their way home and paying less attention to road traffic than they might otherwise. Banning phones may simply result in them being snuck in anyway, which may only increase the risk of loss or misuse.

Age restrictions

Lessons on age restrictions for apps and games are all very well, but mean little or nothing without the backing of parents. Parents may also challenge schools with the response that what goes on at home isn't the business of the headteacher and staff; yet it is the concern of schools, particularly in regard to safeguarding, to behaviour and to bullying. There are occasions when frank and honest conversations will need to take place about inappropriate language and conduct resulting from a child's interaction with social media sites, online chat or computer gaming. Complaints from other parents or children, attention drawn to unsuitable use of certain applications, screenshots of conversations and audio recording of online interaction and inappropriate photographs – all make for uncomfortable conversations but ones we must have, once aware of them.

For those unfamiliar with age restrictions, at the time of going to press these were as follows:

- **Instagram, Facebook, Twitter, Snapchat:** 13 years of age.
- **YouTube:** Account holders need to be 18 years and over, but with parental permission, accounts can be held from the age of 13.
- **WhatsApp:** 16 years of age.

PEGI (Pan European Game Information) ratings place computer games into one of six age categories: 3, 7, 12, 16 and 18. This is not dissimilar to ratings of films in the cinema in terms of their language, violence, drugs and sexual references. However, without firm controls at home, these restrictions are often not followed. For example, there are 18-rated games that children openly talk of playing but when raised with parents, the responses are on the lines of: 'It's OK, he plays it with his dad!' or 'They only play it on the TV, not in their rooms.' In fact, the language and actions from the game are repeated on the playground, meaning it is far from acceptable.

Merely preaching about age restrictions to children, particularly as they get older, more confident and more willing to push boundaries, is likely to fall upon deaf ears. They do need to hear stories, be told of real-life examples and see the modelling of good behaviours in online interactions. Blocking access to gaming sites in school is essential; children do try to log onto them on school devices, and sometimes seemingly innocent-looking sites have links to chat room spaces. There are even instances of games that have been accessed and reprogrammed by hackers so the language becomes offensive and threatening.

Peer pressure

Peer pressure has changed in the online and digital world. Children cannot leave behind their peers at 3.30 pm if they are in contact through a game or an app. Whilst it could be argued that interacting with friends over a game, through headsets and chat facilities, can improve a child's social and communication skills, it can also lead to aggression and short tempers, as well as bullying behaviours for making a perceived 'mistake' on the game. When these behaviours manifest themselves in school, then those crucial communication skills aren't top of our priority list.

The instant access to information and gossip that devices provide have led to a fear of missing out (FOMO, for those unfamiliar with the term), which is true for adults as much as children. Whilst, as adults, we can self-regulate our use of screen time, children find this more of a challenge. When children are allowed devices in their own room, particularly overnight, the temptation is too close. Peer pressure to be involved in activities such as a Snapchat chain challenge, passing on a photo of a blank screen and keeping the chain going as long as possible, can run into the early hours. The 'who can stay up the latest' challenge, set up on a group chat, has a direct impact on the classroom, with late arrivals, weary eyes and children falling asleep on their desks.

Apps that involve group chats, of which WhatsApp is the most prevalent, can be highly problematic. Even as adults, we know that a group with several members can become quite insular, secretive or toxic; adults have the choice to mute or leave, but children may be more reluctant. Feeling that they are away from adult eyes, children may take more risks with their language and content than they would around school or in the company of their parents. They may also be exposed to sexualised language and the use of the emoji to convey certain messages; it doesn't take much imagination to think of what an aubergine emoji means, or a banana, two cherries or a peach. One temptation on such chats is for children to discuss the adults in school, perhaps in disrespectful terms.

The group chat, particularly on WhatsApp, has another, less obvious hazard. In adding contacts to a group, all members then know the phone numbers of all participants. Most of us would only offer our phone number to someone we would wish to have a conversation with. If children add outsiders to their group chats, the sharing of phone numbers without permission potentially exposes children to some degree of risk, of unwanted contact or maybe of bullying.

Another danger of peer pressure, and a fear of parents, is the taking of inappropriate pictures and how quickly they can be shared. This is illustrated perfectly in the NSPCC short film 'I Saw Your Willy', in which Alex is persuaded by his friend to pose for a picture, of which a screengrab is taken and shared, firstly around school but then more widely. At one minute in length, the film turns from a tone of mild amusement to one that is dark and disturbing, to illustrate the dangers, fear and impact that such actions can have on a number of people.

Sexting, the sending of explicit messages and pictures, particularly on a livestream, has become an emergent concern in recent years, and this is not an issue confined to secondary pupils; increasingly, parents of primary-aged children are expressing concern at this risk. Peer pressure, threats, blackmail and self-esteem may all be reasons for such behaviour and, as part of safeguarding, it's important to have steps in place in case such an incident should arise.

How do we, as teachers, know these things happen? We know because there are parents who check their children's phones, who screenshot their concerns and tell schools about what concerns them. There are parents who track their children's use of their phones. When schools hear of these concerns, we have another aspect of safeguarding that requires addressing and needs some difficult conversations with parents.

Parental engagement

Undoubtedly, one of the biggest issues in dealing with e-safety is engaging parents. Many readers will have had the experience of holding parent forums on digital safety, only to find the few attendees were those parents who attend everything and tend to be highly supportive in any case, or that attendance is zero.

One issue, particularly in regard to the use of platforms such as Facebook, is parental attitude to their own use of social media. We may be familiar with the sight of screenshots brought in by concerned parents of unpleasant and hurtful comments about the school or individual teachers, or even about children. Dealing with this can be a challenge; we do not, after all, have any jurisdiction over parents, who may simply respond to being spoken to about this in quite blunt terms. Similarly, when word leaks to teachers of what is being discussed on class WhatsApp groups, more upset can follow.

The simplest way of getting parents to engage in the digital experience is to use a little 'cloak and dagger' style of subtlety. Use of the Friday Celebration Assembly, which parents regularly attend, is one such way. By keeping the children back in class for a short time, there is a captive audience of parents and the opportunity to inform and educate.

Feeding back a survey of children's attitudes to online life can be a wake-up call to parents. Children are very open and honest to hands-up surveys. Try these questions:

- Who has their own mobile phone or tablet?
- Who has been online when their adult is out of the room?
- Who has played a game rated 12 or 18?
- Who uses WhatsApp?
- Who has their own social media account?
- Who has ever 'chatted' with someone online whom they didn't know in real life?
- Who has been worried by or scared of something they have seen online, but not told their parents?

Be prepared for parents to watch aghast. The availability of reliable broadband and of mobile data can allow a child online anywhere in the house. If parents do not have protections in place, children are potentially a click away from the insidious side of life online. Sometimes we need to be this blunt in our language to make our point. We may also need to direct parents to real-life events.

Breck Bednar

Breck Bednar was a 14-year-old schoolboy with a passionate interest in online gaming, something he engaged in with a group of friends after school, a group that was exclusive and controlled by another member whom none of the others had met.

Breck's mother, Lorin LaFave, became suspicious of this older boy and tried to limit Breck's access to his gaming devices. She was concerned about changes in his behaviour and personality, believing this to have been influenced by the group leader, and also raised concerns with the police about online grooming.

Without his parents' knowledge, Breck travelled to the home of the older boy. Here he was murdered. Images were posted online before the police arrived. A 19-year-old man was arrested and charged, admitting his guilt before a jury could be sworn in.

Lorin LaFave speaks openly and eloquently about her experience and of how, even as a parent who tried to put controls in place and had raised her concerns with authority, she was unable to prevent the tragic death of her son. She has established The Breck Foundation in his memory to campaign to ensure that children are not put at risk whilst they use the internet.

Sharing Breck Bednar's story with parents will emphasise the need for control and monitoring of their child's online activity, but this is a message that needs to be constantly drip-fed to parents, particularly in relation to age restrictions.

Gaming is a particular area of concern. Primary-aged children should not be downloading or playing Fortnite, with a suggested age limit of 12, yet a simple glance at the brand on children's lunchboxes says that they do. The aggressive language, 'trash talk' and violence can be repeated on the playground and can lead to some difficult conversations with parents in confronting an issue about something the children might do outside of school.

E-safety in the National Curriculum

In the curriculum for computing, it is stated that schools should aim for children to be responsible, competent, confident and creative users of information and communication technology. The subject content says that children in Key Stage 1 should know how to use computers safely and respectfully, how to keep personal information secret and where to go for help or support. At Key Stage 2, this is extended to the recognition and reporting of unacceptable behaviour and of knowing what acceptable online behaviour looks like.

Teaching of safety is explicitly stated and therefore needs to be part of a regular diet of the computing curriculum, not saved for a focused day or week. Educating children, and parents, about how to use the Childline freephone number, the Child Exploitation and Online Protection website (part of the National Crime Agency) and the online support provided by the London Grid for Learning (LGFL Digisafe) should be a priority and be available through every communication platform the school has, either online or on paper.

Suggested learning opportunities and activities for e-safety

Many of these activities, particularly in EYFS, are recommended to be shared with parents, as the bulk of the children's experiences online are likely to be at home and outside of school. Let the children, and their parents, know that everything on the internet could be seen by anyone in the world. The best emphasis is on safety, prevention and responsibility rather than on danger.

EYFS	• Teach the children how to log on to a computer as early as possible, ideally once they have an understanding of their letters and can enter their name on a keyboard. • Teach the children what we mean by personal information, perhaps through the use of a puppet who will be playing the role of a trusted adult. The children may tell the puppet their name, age, favourite colour and so on. Replace the puppet with an unknown puppet; if they start to tell the new puppet something, the trusted adult puppet can intervene and stop them sharing. Link this to being safe around strangers. • Ask children to name and draw their trusted adults. • Introduce internet safety rules at the earliest opportunity and pass these up as the children grow through the school and their understanding of being safe develops.

KS1	• Introduce email to the children, as a way of sending a message quickly. • Link the idea of email to politeness and model a greeting and sign-off. • Teach that, even though an email is a message to one person, it might be seen by others because it can be copied and forwarded. • Be explicit in teaching never to put online something you would not say out loud. • Teach about the implications of inappropriate online searches and how these can lead to upsetting images and messages on screen. Teach the children what to do if they see this: tell an adult who will report it.
LKS2	• Discuss the importance of having a secure password. As a school, be in the habit of changing passwords to access the school system and all applications on an annual basis. Though this can create a few problems with adults and children remembering passwords, doing so can enable this to become a lifetime habit. • Teach the children ways of reporting online concerns themselves and that there is a trusted adult monitoring and acting upon those concerns. • Ask the children to think about communicating and modelling safe habits around the school (see the section on digital leaders in Chapter 10, page 148). The children could produce presentations for children, parents and governors.
UKS2	• Teach the importance of online privacy and how to be safe and respectful of others online. • Agree a set of online safety rules and amend this through the year as children become aware of new technologies and applications. • Set up some online or real-life role play situations, where the lead character faces moral dilemmas based on the activity or encouragement of others.

An e-safety assembly

There are a vast number of e-safety assemblies available online, from the UK Safer Internet Centre and on the websites of individual schools, as well as those shared on teacher resource websites. This one has been written with the experience of online lessons in mind.

Preparation

On your presentation slides, have some pictures that look like they are selfies or taken from an online video meeting application. If using pictures of people, use library stock photographs taken from the web; never use pictures of staff in an assembly shared online or as part of the school website, as this would actually be counter to the content of this assembly.

Assembly music

'Who Do You Share Your Details With?' by the News Kids on the Block, a parody of a One Direction song performed by CBBC presenters, is a catchy but powerful reminder of keeping safe online.

Setting the scene

Ask the children whether they have heard of the following behaviours online or know what they mean:

- **Trolling:** Someone saying unkind or untrue things about someone on the internet.
- **Going viral:** When a picture or post gets thousands of views all around the world, this is known as *going viral*. This discussion might lead to some explanation about computer viruses and human viruses too.
- **Meme:** When an online picture is used to make fun of someone or something.
- **Griefing:** When someone on a game like Minecraft or Roblox deliberately spoils your creation or steals your equipment.

Though the children might not know the terms, they might understand and recognise the scenarios.

Moving on

Sharing photographs online

Raise the following discussion points with the children:

- If I post a photo on the internet, who can see it?
- If I post a photo of myself on the internet and someone says something untrue or unkind, what could I do?
- If I'm speaking to someone online, are they actually the person I think they are?

Hopefully the children will recognise that anyone can see anything on the internet. They may not know that they can report something untrue or unkind to the NSPCC or Child Exploitation and Online Protection Centre (CEOP), but ideally they will answer that they can tell a teacher or parent. The third question is trickier; some children will know that people can pretend to be someone else online. However, many will not, because it is something that does come from experience and perhaps they may have been shielded from this by cautious parents. Equally, their naivety or curiosity might potentially have led them into a conversation with a stranger.

Personal information

Ask the children what they understand by personal information. Should this information ever be shared?

The answer to the first question should relate to something that identifies a person: name, gender, school, address, age. The answer to the second should be a very firm 'no' if the children have had a regular dose of internet safety advice in previous years.

Be share aware

In this part of the assembly, talk about why the children should never have their school uniform in a photo other than a school photo. Talk about other things that shouldn't be shared, such as pictures of houses, which might give away door numbers, pictures of friends taken on the way home and even photos of cats and dogs.

Should you share a password?

Again, the children should know not to share a password, but explain to them that many passwords can be easily guessed because birthdays, pet names and house numbers often feature in vulnerable passwords.

Online respect

Discuss with the children why we need to be respectful online and how saying something hurtful or rude can humiliate other people. Go on to talk about respecting ourselves online; if the children were asked to do something they didn't like, would they do it?

Two good rules to remember to show respect online

Firstly, never say anything that wouldn't be said to an actual person in real life, and secondly, never post a picture or a video of something we wouldn't like to see printed on a poster or a t-shirt.

Know who you're talking to

Not everyone tells the truth online. Someone who says they're eight years old and called Alex may not be who they say they are. There is only one rule here; do not talk to, share photos with or agree to meet someone you don't know in real life.

Reflection

Ask the children for all the good things about the internet. Then ask them what some of the bad things are. Emphasise that we do not want to scare children away from the internet but there are things we need to do to be cautious. Ask the children for one thing that they would like to change about the internet.

Follow-up

Make sure that these discussions are followed up in class and that teachers and teaching assistants are open to listening to the worries that children have about online use. Share concerns with parents in general terms as part of ongoing good practice around computer safety.

Postscript: e-safety, lockdown learning and digital overload

As this book was nearing completion, the United Kingdom entered a third pandemic lockdown, which completely changed the face of teaching in this country. Overnight, we became a profession that taught remotely, with a mixture of live and recorded lessons supplemented with a diet of Oak Academy and BBC Bitesize.

Instantaneously, the message that we had given, or even preached, to our children and their parents about limiting time online was overturned, with the Department for Education directing schools to provide up to four hours of online learning for families who had again found themselves marooned in their homes at short notice.

Though schools had been anticipating possible short-term provision of remote, digital teaching, the challenge from the classroom was matched, if not exceeded, by that in the home. The limited availability of devices, wi-fi capacity at full stretch if parents and secondary siblings were working from home, and the ability of parents and families to support their youngest offspring in these most unusual of circumstances represented just a few aspects of challenge to family wellbeing. The additional burden on families was now the expectation that children completed the work set; the prospect of a call from the school about non-engagement was probably not helping their wellbeing. The weight of expectation on schools to maintain the curriculum provision, suspended in the original lockdown, placed a further obstacle in the way of teachers, already facing having a larger number of key worker children in their classrooms than previously.

In terms of digital wellbeing, the principal problem arising from Lockdown Mark III was the sheer amount of time that children were facing a screen. A family with two children and only one device would have been online for around six to eight hours a day, aside from the time that parents might have been engaged in their work from home. Simply staring at a screen for that length of time in a day isn't healthy in the workplace. For children, however much they love working on a computer, this was simply exhausting – a different kind of exhaustion than a 'normal' day in school would have resulted in. If teachers were expressing how much their eyes hurt from looking at a laptop all day, we can only speculate how our pupils must have felt. Engaging with, at worst, a disembodied voice or, at best, a slightly grainy image of a face that would have been so familiar only weeks before may have been an adventure for a few days, but after half a term, it had become wearing on the patience and resilience of the children.

An aspect of e-safety we had probably not considered before was how much children were able to keep up with the pace of lessons online. In class in 'usual' circumstances, we pause, question, reflect and often divert from the lesson in hand as we meet the needs of our young learners. The nuances of the classroom, how we respond to the look of the child who hasn't quite understood the concept or to the probing questions that children are so adept at asking, be it an extension of or distraction from learning, were suddenly absent. Children thrive on this in the classroom, so once faced with a situation where they are 'muted' or relying on a chat facility to interact with their teachers, they are away from a familiar comfort zone and dependent upon the skill of the now remote teacher or the adult they may, or may not, be with at home to guide them. The degree of uncertainty that these children must have felt can be measured in the relative quality of the work they subsequently produced.

A further risk of being online through the course of what would have been a school day is the ever-present temptation of other uses of digital platforms. In school, we actively teach children to open a different tab and to switch between them as part of internet research. In our IT suites, there will have been any number of children who may have flipped onto a tab with a video or gaming, but have been caught out by an eagle-eyed teacher or a software package that alerts the school to any access to unsuitable sites. At home, there is no such protection, other than the attention of a parent. Children looking for a distraction from the rigours of remote learning might have been tempted, if parental attention was not fully upon them, to look elsewhere online. Being online for such a period of time can result in dependency on a device, and the ease of flipping from an educational use of a computer to an inappropriate and potentially dangerous site has shown that online learning may not have been the idyll that some imagined.

*

E-safety could very easily look like the stern adult lecturing the disinterested child, and if we are having to deal with incidents in school, we must wonder at times whether we are being listened to. It remains an important part of our safeguarding responsibility. We should never lay off the subject; we just need to think smart. This smart thinking needs the teacher to show an awareness of what the children might be using and being aware of some of the language that might be associated with gaming and other online activity. National providers, such as the NSPCC and LGfL, provide regular updates and there are subscription services to which schools can sign up. When talking about e-safety becomes the norm, rather than a one-off event, it builds into the culture of safety that we would all like to see.

Success criteria: What does a school that prioritises e-safety look like?

- Children have an awareness of their digital dependency and the impact it has on their language, behaviour and social interaction.
- Children consider how to use a device safely before getting caught up in the status that a new generation of phone brings.
- All adults fully understand why there are age limits and realise the potential risks involved.
- Children resist peer pressure through their digital experience.
- The school engages parents in a non-judgemental and supportive manner.
- Children know where to turn to when they are worried or threatened by what they see online.

8 Cyberbullying

Chapter overview

This chapter will discuss the nature of cyberbullying, and some of the problems associated with it in relation to children in primary school. We will define cyberbullying, in terms of what we may encounter in the primary school and what our children might experience outside of school. We will consider ways of teaching about cyberbullying and the impact it can have on people, both as victims and as perpetrators. Prevention and intervention are presented as possible strategies alongside modelling of healthy online behaviours in the classroom, which we would like to see continued as the children go online at home.

Cyberbullying is a scourge of twenty-first-century society, encouraged sadly by the availability of and instant gratification brought by high-speed internet access. Anyone who is a user of social media will have been aware of terms such as trolling, sealioning, gaslighting and pile-ons. For those unfamiliar with these terms, here are some brief definitions:

- **Trolling:** The intentional causing of upset by posting inflammatory, controversial or attention-seeking comments online or in response to another post. (You will remember that this term was touched upon in the assembly in the previous chapter.)

- **Sealioning:** The confrontational practice of jumping into an online discussion with demands for answers and evidence, aimed to erode the patience, attention and resilience of the target.
- **Gaslighting:** A specific form of manipulation and control where the target has their sense of reality and memory questioned.
- **Pile-on:** A rapidly growing attack on one target, often deliberately generated by another user with a larger audience.

As an adult, careful curation of our timelines, blocking, muting and taking digital detox breaks helps with our digital wellbeing. For a child, this is new ground, rife with temptation and pitfalls. This temptation, coupled with a potential lack of self-awareness, lays bare the possibility of joining a thread or a conversation that could lead them into deep trouble, whilst also seriously impacting upon the wellbeing of the recipient.

Cyberbullying is bullying that takes place online and, unlike more conventional 'playground bullying', it can follow a child around, through social media networks, gaming, online chat and smartphones. Again, as in the previous chapter, digital dangers are lurking in the home environment. Many of us will have dealt with screenshots of incidents timed in the evening, weekend or holidays. There may also be a lack of parental supervision or awareness that such conduct is being played out under their roof. It may be the case that children become so wrapped up in their digital world that the language and actions of cyberbullying become embedded. As one respondent to my research told me:

> *'In certain classes, it doesn't matter who comes to speak to them (teacher, head, police); they just are so wrapped up in being online that your messages don't get through. There is no support from home.'*

The nature of cyberbullying and the ready access that children have to the world of digital interaction mean that, whilst some parents might not appear supportive, there will be many others unaware of the activities in which their child may be engaging. The difficulty we have in primary school is that policing something outside of school times is outside our remit until it starts impacting life in the classroom. Even then, a response of 'you can't tell my child what they can or cannot do outside of school' may be heard. In some ways this parent may be correct, but on the other hand if we in the primary sector don't address the issue at its source through the strength of our character education, then children's awareness of their actions and responsibilities as they move into secondary education may be clouded.

Types of cyberbullying

Cyberbullying can include activity and messaging on any online platform. The perpetrator might be involved in any of the following behaviours.

The sending of threatening or abusive text messages

Usually on a one-on-one basis, this behaviour is particularly threatening as it can come at any time of the day, often at night. With many children keeping their device with them overnight in the privacy of their bedroom, this represents not only an invasion of privacy but also an intimidating incursion into sleep patterns and the recipient's individual time and space.

Creating and sharing embarrassing images or videos

The availability of photo manipulation software, much of it free to download, allows for easy and quick adaptations to be made to existing photographs; indeed, this is something we may teach within our computing lessons. Filters, which smartphone cameras have and which are used in many applications, allow for enhancements to pictures to be made instantaneously. Within seconds, it is possible to send such images to a group and to a further network. This is most startlingly demonstrated in the NSPCC video I mentioned in the previous chapter, 'I Saw Your Willy', which, through brevity and carefully targeted humour, shows the speed at which an image can be spread.

Trolling

As defined at the beginning of this chapter, trolling is the sending of menacing or upsetting messages on social networks, chat rooms or online games. This will be familiar to many readers, particularly regular users of social platforms. The language used is often framed in a way that shames the recipient, encourages others to join in and is designed to portray an image of the victim that is an offensive misrepresentation of them, or patently untrue.

Excluding children from online games, activities or friendship groups

Though we have age-inappropriate games being played by primary-aged children, as detailed in Chapter 7, there are also games that are often regarded as educationally beneficial in terms of their IT skills and knowledge (Minecraft and Roblox come to mind) but that have the potential to allow for social exclusion. The setting up of groups is comparatively straightforward, and even if the children play in a closed group of their classmates, the setting up of sub-groups to play or chat is an easy step to make. There is a distinct imbalance between a group to discuss strategy and one to discuss targeting another child. Activity included within this definition also covers changing passwords of other children, accessing their accounts and sending inappropriate messages from that account.

Shaming someone online

This usually manifests itself through supposedly age-restricted social networks, where an image or comment posted is then seen not only by the network, but theoretically by a global audience. The addition of a hashtag or of an oft-searched keyword makes the potential discovery of this, by those wishing to harm children, a distinct possibility.

Sexting and pressuring children into sending sexual images

Sexting is the sending of a sexual message and/or a naked or semi-naked image, video or text message to another person. Though we might think this is more of a risk in secondary school as adolescence kicks in, there is increasing concern for primary-aged children. Indeed, reference to it should be included in the safeguarding policy. Whilst there may be a degree of consent, there may also be a larger element of coercion. There is also no control over how that image is subsequently used once posted. It is a criminal offence to create or share such images, even if the person doing so is a child. Despite the reticence some schools might have in dealing with cyberbullying outside of school, this is one area where we have to act and liaise with other childcare professionals.

Other types of cyberbullying

Although the following are often associated with secondary schools, the ease with which they could be set up needs to be within our thinking in the primary sector:

- Setting up groups encouraging hateful discussion about a particular child. Be aware that this can also include parents.
- Encouraging young people to self-harm.
- Voting for or against someone in an abusive poll.
- Creating fake accounts and misrepresenting online identities to embarrass a child or cause trouble using their name.

Prevention or cure?

Children love a visitor assembly, especially when the guest can push the boundaries with the children in a way the headteacher wouldn't dare. An effective assembly or class presentation makes a point, and where this is positive, it can spur the children to action; climate change, single-use plastics and campaigns against littering all come to mind. These draw from the moral integrity and moral character that good character promotes. Other themes in this book address positive aspects of character and wellbeing. There is nothing positive or character-forming about cyberbullying. Yet we need to cover this topic, make children aware of it and give them strategies to deal with it when it happens.

As a starting point, rather than teach that cyberbullying goes on, the first lessons in this topic should be positive and healthy online habits, without even a mention of the word 'cyberbullying' until the end of Key Stage 2. Think about the water safety assembly that each year rightly highlights the dangers of swimming in quarries, docks, ponds and rivers; even though the assembly makes it clear that these are hazardous areas, it may have the unwanted side effect of placing the thought in the minds of our young people that these might be somewhere for them to go. To ask a child not to do something might be a temptation too far. Similarly, with the concept of cyberbullying, approaching it from the negative side first may unwittingly encourage participation in such activity.

As a positive platform to begin from, we don't need to mention smartphones, computers or digital interaction; we start as we did in previous chapters with the school culture and how we speak to and interact with different people. Try, for example, showing an image of someone with wildly coloured or styled hair – a 1970s punk rocker is a good example. After the initial giggles, which are a natural response of children to someone looking so different, invite the children to talk about what might be said to this person. Adapt these questions to match the age and responses of the children:

- Do you find this person funny or are you scared of them?
- What might you say about their hair?
- Does this sound rude? Or impolite?
- Can you change what you have said?
- Did you need to say anything in the first place?

The final question can be an opportunity to address the point at which natural curiosity crosses into inappropriate interaction or rudeness. Recently, I showed my Year 6 class a clip from *The Elephant Man*, where John Merrick is making his way through a crowded railway station and, though hooded, is seemingly unnoticed by his fellow travellers. A young boy, perhaps looking for trouble, spots Merrick, harasses him and as he tries to escape, the subsequent commotion draws in a crowd that pursues and corners him in a public convenience. Whilst this lesson itself wasn't about cyberbullying, it was an illustrative point as to how something could escalate quickly, involve others and have unpleasant consequences.

As our children develop in their character education, knowing when to say something, and crucially when not to, is a trait of character that needs modelling and good examples set.

Cyberbullying within the National Curriculum

The section on computing in the National Curriculum quite rightly focuses on understanding, analysis, evaluation and application of computer terminology and technology. In the statement about the aims of the computing curriculum is a reference to being a responsible user of information and communication technology. In Key Stage 1, there is a requirement to teach the safe and respectful use of technology and knowing where to go with concerns. This is echoed in Key Stage 2, with the addition of 'responsibly' to the document.

The simple reference to responsibility justifies the coverage of cyberbullying within our wellbeing and character curriculum. We can focus on responsible actions if children are faced with it, managing and responding to peer pressure to be involved in this form of bullying and how to avoid being engaged in this behaviour if involved in it.

Suggested learning opportunities and activities for teaching about cyberbullying

EYFS	• Incorporate all the positive talk opportunities that are promoted in EYFS to promote a culture of care and empathy. As a starting point for healthy and supportive relationships, this is a crucial foundation. • It may not be appropriate to involve any use of technology at this point in time, but it is worth acknowledging that activities that promote empathetic play and interaction, combined with praise and positive modelling, encourage respectful attitudes. • As an introduction to positive online behaviour, the use of positive emojis to express thanks and feelings could be introduced here.

KS1	• Use an online video (such as those provided by the UK Safer Internet Centre) to stimulate discussion and conversation around safe conduct.
	• What could be done if we receive a hurtful message online?
	  ○ Who can we tell at home?
	  ○ Who can we tell at school?
	• Is it acceptable to be mean to someone online?
	• How can we be a good friend online?
	• Using a writing frame of a message box, with limited space, send a message to someone else. Encourage a reply and a 'conversation', then introduce one 'mean' message into the conversation, perhaps scripted by an adult. This can then be used to introduce ways of challenging such behaviour and strategies for escaping from it.
	• Generate a list of the different activities that can be done online. This can be done in class but also by interviewing older children and adults in the school. Ensure children understand that there are many ways of being online that potentially expose them to cyberbullying. Agree a set of rules and actions for what to do in the case of receiving an unpleasant message online, and share this with parents.

LKS2	• Play real-life 'Guess Who?' with the class. Begin with questions like 'Has this person got long hair?' and 'Do they have blue eyes?' Then, with much sensitivity, drop in questions that might have links to other differences, possibly related to playground incidents. Sensitively planned, this is a way into promoting and celebrating difference and is a positive means of addressing some issues that arise through cyberbullying. • Being conscious of safe internet conduct, children write five things that they would be happy to share online. Now they add five things they wouldn't share.
UKS2	• Discuss the ways in which cyberbullying is different to bullying in class, on the playground or on the way home. • Brainstorm examples of this type of bullying behaviour. • Is this type of bullying more or less serious than 'conventional' bullying? Give reasons why. • Does it physically hurt someone? Or does it affect someone emotionally? • Ask children to work in small groups to develop an action plan to consider strategies for what they could do if they suffer this or witness it. • Discuss confidentiality, privacy and online safety. • The old-fashioned game of 'Consequences' could be adapted here, to invite challenging or appropriate responses to an image and to consider feelings and emotional responses to this. • Share anonymous 'impact statements', either imagined or real, if this incident is having to be addressed in school. • Build an element of this into written narratives and fact-based writing. • Draft guidance based on children's responses so that any policy includes the children's voice.

A cyberbullying assembly

To keep a positive approach to the topic that fits the values and culture of the school but shows that we take the subject of cyberbullying seriously, an assembly with an element of interaction, role play and humour can bring this into sharp focus.

Take this as a whole-school, or whole-key-stage or year-group, assembly, with teachers present to aid the interaction for added emphasis and to follow up in class. This assembly works best with interaction because it demonstrates the instantaneous and reactive nature of some responses whilst emphasising the core message of 'think before you post'.

Preparation

This assembly does need to be presented on a screen or interactive whiteboard and will work with any slideshow software. For those feeling brave, you could use a setup that would allow one or more well-briefed colleagues to type live responses to the presenter's words. Otherwise, leaving a presentation clicker with a colleague or one of the children will work just as effectively.

Adapt the script given below as appropriate, but the presenter will need to be in the role of a child to make the point; acting a bit 'street' will add humour and engage the audience. Preparation might involve the wearing of trainers, baseball cap or other items untypical of usual teacher attire. There should be a photograph of you wearing these items on the first slide of the presentation. The rest of the slides should show the script, with each line being brought up by a click of the mouse.

Assembly music

Played before or after the assembly, 'Drift' by Emily Osment from the film *Cyberbully* has very effective visual accompaniment linking the online behaviour to real-life interaction.

Setting the scene

Begin the assembly in your role as a child and say:

> *'Hi everyone! I'm Sam and this morning, I am going to be using my tablet to post some pictures on Snapbook* [or any made-up portmanteau of

social network apps] *so my friends can see just how cool I am. I am going to send them a picture of me in my stylish trainers and baseball cap… here we go, that's a great picture* [bring up the photograph of you wearing your items on the slideshow]. *Now just let me think of some words… I know: "Hey U guys UR not going 2 believe what a DUDE I look like today".*

This will then allow the slides to be played through, with the presenter reading the posts aloud. With a combination of internal monologue and the actual typed response, the children can start to see the impact of the words on the presenter. Replace my non-gender-specific names with your own choice, but not those of children in the school for obvious reasons.

Ally: Top of the class for fashion there, mate! I reckon Stormzy is well jel.

Sam: Thanks sis/bro. You want to chill l8er?

Ally: Homework l8er! Let's hang out online for a while.

Georgie: Homework is for losers! And what do your trainers look like?! Did your dad buy them from the charity shop or did your mum find them in a skip?

Ally: Well, I tell the folks it's homework but they don't check. I'm here all day.

Georgie: Did you see Sam's baseball cap? What loser wears it like that?

Sam internal monologue: I'm not a loser! How horrid. Who invited Georgie to this conversation? I should say something, but Mum said I mustn't say bad things on here, in case someone screenshots it. Here we go.

Sam: Hi Georgie. I saw Stormzy wearing it like that last week. You like him?

Georgie: Stormzy. He is so last year. I reckon you listen to him on CD.

Ally: Yeah! When his/her dad lets him/her!

Georgie: I wouldn't want Sam's dad's waxy ear buds!

Ally: They listen to music on a gramophone in that house! Probably have to wind it up!

Sam internal monologue: What is Ally up to? I thought they liked me.

Sam: Hey Ally. That's not fair. You've been to my house loads of times.

Georgie: Listen to the cry baby! In the class chat they all say your mum buys your trainers off the market.

Continue this as long as you feel appropriate, being aware of your audience and how they may respond. Build the assembly to this story climax.

Sam: I don't like what you two are saying on here. It is making me really uncomfortable and embarrassed.

Ally: This isn't Ally. It is Ally's mum. Ally left his/her tablet on the kitchen table just now and I have seen what has been said here. Georgie has done this to other people in the class too. The parent group has had complaints about this, because there has been talk about things happening in school, but now I can believe this for myself. I have screenshotted this conversation. This is cyberbullying. I will be speaking to Georgie's parents and bringing this up with the school too.

Reflection

Draw responses from the children on these points. Depending on your audience, or the context of your school and study, this is something the teachers may want to do in class as a follow-up.

- How has Sam acted sensibly and responsibly?
- What has Georgie done that is wrong?
- What has Ally done that is wrong?
- What do you think the school will do?
- What could Sam or Ally have done to stop this getting out of their control?
- How did each participant feel in the course of this exchange?

Follow-up

- In class, you may wish to talk through or role-play the conversation with a 'think before you post' emphasis, particularly for Ally and the peer pressure from Georgie to join in.
- Other learning points can be drawn from what the consequences are for Sam, particularly if this had been a repeated pattern of behaviour, and whether Ally had been involved in this before as a follower or had been a target.
- A thought-provoking line of discussion could come through how Georgie should be dealt with, how the character might be sanctioned and how to persuade them not to continue in this vein.

Parental engagement

Though the majority of cyberbullying incidents, as for e-safety occurrences, will happen outside of school, once they impact on children and their fears for their own safety, then schools do need to address the matter. In approaching parents, in a similar way to children, commencing from a preventative point of view and building on the good relationships between families and schools is preferable to a more reactive approach should an incident occur. Here are some specific strategies to try.

Inform parents

Children are obtaining smartphones at increasingly younger ages. Education of parents through workshops, newsletters, and online and real-life meetings will allow them to be informed of what cyberbullying is and how it might be prevented.

Encourage monitoring of their children's devices

A range of software is available to track phones and to monitor how they are being used. The simplest monitoring is of course physically inspecting the phone and the history of each application. Having a shared and agreed space where devices can be charged or kept overnight also promotes healthy habits and digital-device-free time.

Teach parents about the use of social media

Some parents are well versed in the use of social media platforms, but many won't be. Instructional video or other presentations can be used to illustrate safe and purposeful use of social media alongside promotion of reasons why there are age limit guidelines on their use. If, as a school, you are able to have regular parent workshops, this is an ideal opportunity for parents to raise concerns in a non-judgemental arena. Sadly, there will be parents and older siblings who get involved in such activity themselves; where this impacts on school life, it is a matter for the headteacher and senior leaders to address.

Teach parents the signs of cyberbullying

Parents know their children and know the way they behave. They notice changes in behaviour, which could be related to cyberbullying but not exclusively so. Some key signs to look out for in identifying whether children are being bullied include:

- loss of appetite
- loss of interest in previously enjoyed activities
- school avoidance tactics such as feigned illness
- lack of engagement with family activities.

More specific to cyberbullying might be these signs:

- secretive behaviours, such as hiding phones or devices
- a noticeable change, increased or reduced, in the amount of time spent on devices
- refusal to show devices to parents and deletion of messages.

Parents may also wish to know if their child is leading the cyberbullying. This is a problematic area, as many parents may not wish to acknowledge that their child is involved in this behaviour. Kindness, patience and consistency would be the best advice here. Typical conduct for parents to be aware of include:

- hiding their phone from an adult or sibling, often when suddenly disturbed
- opening multiple social media accounts for one platform using anonymised names
- being aggressive, defensive or upset if a parent asks to look at the phone
- blocking a parent from following their social media accounts
- mood changes
- making sarcastic or nasty remarks about other people when they think a parent can't hear them.

These may make for challenging conversations in a school, but I believe that establishing a culture of open and honest conversation around the topic will make dealing with such circumstances, should they arise, much easier to address.

Success criteria: What does a school that prioritises tackling cyberbullying look like?

- Children recognise cyberbullying. They recognise if it is happening to them or to someone else and have strategies to challenge it or deal with it.
- Children acknowledge if they have engaged in some activities and find ways to avoid them in future or to seek help for their own safety.
- Children acknowledge that participation in cyberbullying does not make someone fundamentally 'bad' and that they are capable of change.
- All children, whether victim, bystander, witness or perpetrator, learn from and act upon what has happened.

9 Building trust

Chapter overview

In this chapter, we will consider how trust can be built and grown, embedded and supported, but also broken and exploited.

Areas discussed

Learning opportunities and activities

Assembly theme

The purpose of school is to develop a place where all children can learn at high levels of attainment and progress, but in order to achieve this they must establish meaningful relationships. This has already been discussed in previous chapters. Trust is an essential component of a meaningful learning relationship, because trust means safety and comfort and a feeling that an individual has support and backing when they need it. In a trusting environment, we can all be our best selves. Building trust is a process, the end goal of which is one where we can have a collective and honest dialogue between children and teachers, between children and parents, and amongst children themselves. In the same way that teachers develop trusting relationships with their colleagues, the model that we need to create for our children is one that will enable them to build the same trusting relationships with each other and with the adults they encounter.

Trust is an abstract principle, but you don't have to be special to build trust. The most important thing for a person to show is that they are prepared to invest time in building relationships. Structuring our time management to ensure that we show our appreciation for our children is one such approach that can build trust. As was discussed in Chapter 2, positive interactions relating to behaviour can have a huge impact upon the relationship the teacher has with the child and with their parents. In taking some time to ensure that, in discussing the growth of our pupils, we look not only at their academic progress but at their character development as well, we show an appreciation of the whole child.

There is huge importance in covering trust through our direct and indirect teaching, as trust forms such a key part of relationships education and in recognising, building and maintaining trustful and respectful relationships. Through everyday activities, focused lessons and impromptu responses to unforeseen changes, schools can embed trust within their PSHE provision and in the broader curriculum.

This chapter concludes our section on knowing others. In showing trust of other people, we can show that we have developed strong relationships. We can also think about how the child develops resilience in the face of misplaced trust because this can be potentially harmful if it goes wrong, particularly if the child loses trust in a peer or in an adult.

What does trust look like?

When I have asked children, in class or in assembly, to tell me what they understand by 'trust' or what it looks like, the following answers are typical:

- 'Someone you trust keeps their promises.'
- 'If you trust someone, you feel safe with them.'
- 'Trusting another person means that you believe what they say.'

It is possible to view such answers as the innocence of children, but equally to regard them as a sign of vulnerability. In reality, both are true and trust forms an important starting point for discussion. When developed as a school value, trust can also be a way of exploring other topics, for example the exploration of 'fake news' with older pupils, through stories with younger children, such as *The Gingerbread Man*, or in PE, where a measure of trust is shown in teammates.

Trust and respect: partners in wellbeing and character

Trust and respect are two important and interdependent components of the classroom learning environment. If a child doesn't respect and trust their teacher or if an adult is perceived as being disrespectful in the way they speak or respond to a child's work, the learning environment won't be as nurturing as it ought to be and the teacher's classroom management strategy won't be as effective. A lack of trust and respect can also cause children to feel unsafe and uncomfortable in the classroom, which could have consequences for behaviour management.

Some teachers may think that trust and respect in school settings should be a given expectation, but we need to realise that it does take work to develop trust and nourish respect in the classroom. As we know, the direct or indirect experience that some of our children have of abuse, violence or neglect, or the message that society and the media give of the world being a dangerous place, can leave young people without trust and wary of the environment they encounter.

It takes time to develop trust and respect in the classroom, so it requires the teacher and other adults in the room to help facilitate the process. Being consistent and nurturing are two important qualities and values that we can employ to help the children to develop trust and feel safe in their working space. When we send our PGCE and BEd students or our new and recently qualified teachers to observe more experienced colleagues in their classrooms, it is important to look not only at the 'what, how and why' of the teaching but also at the classroom management in the room. How a teaching assistant is deployed, how the room is organised, how every person in the room speaks to and interacts with each other – all of these build into creating a culture of trust and respect in the class. Below we will look at ways to grow this culture.

Provide a safe and secure environment

Safety and security begin for the children in their immediate environment and this can come from how the classroom is organised. Ensuring that all of children's basic needs are met can provide this security that enables children to explore and participate in active learning. In a well-organised Early Years lesson, which to a non-expert looks like noisy play, children can choose their learning experiences, some of which are directed by adults but many of which are child-initiated. This can become a safe place to take risks, make mistakes and learn from them. Here a child-based environment that features developmentally appropriate materials, activities and techniques can help trust and respect to develop and flourish in the classroom.

Take these principles forward into Key Stages 1 and 2, and even though classrooms look very different, the security of the place the children find themselves in is just as important. Whether seated in rows or groups, it is the organisation of the classroom that enables children to access the resources and support they need and create a positive classroom culture. It is these classrooms that supply or PPA (planning, preparation and assessment) cover teachers appreciate most, as the trust is established by the secure environment.

Encourage positive relationships

Positive relationships in the classroom are in many ways imperative for effective learning and behaviour. Positive relationships also have an impact on children's resilience and can help them to deal with academic and other challenges, hence the importance of teaching the meaning of friendship and looking after each other, discussed in Chapter 6. The model for positive relationships should be driven by adults in the classroom and how they respond to behaviour. Take, for example, a child who calls out: do we respond with 'Don't shout out!' or with 'Thank you for your answer, but could you raise your hand next time?' Which of these is more positive and which classroom will have the greater sense of mutual trust?

Positive relationships can be supported by positive interactions, because these strengthen the child–teacher relationship. The last thing a teacher wants to hear from a parent is that their child feels that the teacher doesn't like them. This can often arise from an unhealthy imbalance between positive and negative interactions, the negative ones often related to behaviour. 'Praise in public, rebuke in private' is oft-heard but sound advice; the teachers with the best discipline are frequently those who don't raise their voices, but remain calm and consistent. All interactions serve to strengthen or challenge classroom relationships, but it may take several positive ones to balance one negative, hence the need for consistency. The positive ones need to be genuine too; a reward for sitting up straight is no reward. As we discussed in Chapter 2, children can see through a contrived merit.

The model of the positive child–teacher relationship is the way to build trusting relationships between children, which comes from ensuring they have the opportunity to work with children other than their friends and to have respect for the abilities of others built into their learning experiences. Striking a balance between choosing their own partners or groups for activities and teacher-directed grouping shows a respect for the children's choices, but also shows the children they need to demonstrate appropriate learning behaviours to maintain the trust of their teachers. Learning how to work with others, how to win with grace and lose with honour, and how to learn that loss doesn't mean failure – these are built into trusting classroom cultures. The relationships children have with other children in and beyond the classroom will also impact trust and respect in their daily experience. Including trust activities in lesson plans is a great way to help students to develop trust in their teacher and classmates. Falling backward, sculpturing and mirroring are three examples of trust activities children will enjoy completing.

One way to start supporting more positive interactions is to regularly evaluate and celebrate the trust and respect in the classroom. Through 'circle time' or other regular class discussion time, a repeated item can be 'Who has shown they have been trusted this week?', as well as how trust has been shown. These discussions can be built into the classroom routine through the use of positive language and examples relating to learning time and to interactions with other children and adults during breaks.

What to do when trust breaks down

Part of our pastoral role will include times when the children feel that trust has broken down. Sadly, this is going to be a life lesson, as we have all in our lives had times where our trust has been betrayed or broken. For children, their experience might be in a broken friendship, and though this may hurt, typically it doesn't last long. We should never be flippant about this, though, and should look to have in place procedures for conflict resolution. Midday staff and teaching assistants, often one and the same, are excellent practitioners in this regard, and with appropriate training it is possible for children to do likewise in solving conflicts between younger children. We need to be mindful of how we support friendship disputes, as these sometimes result in concerns about bullying, which is addressed in Chapter 6.

Often children's most challenging experience will come in the case of family breakdown, where the trust they might have in a loved one could be shattered. This is why we as a school community need to know our families well and to understand that even in break-ups that appear amicable, there is much going on under the surface that children will find difficult to comprehend and to articulate. Some of our families will be open and approach the school directly, but others will be less trusting, particularly if they are suspicious of authority in any way. Whichever the case, we need to suspend judgement in order to place the wellbeing of our children at the forefront of everything we stand for.

When children feel trust has broken down, this is a time when they can become vulnerable to possible exploitation, by bullies or by those seeking to recruit them into gangs or political extremism. Whilst it is unlikely that primary-aged children would join such groups, the vulnerabilities that are exposed may start to become apparent. The child who suddenly becomes very quiet, or unusually verbally or physically aggressive; the one who develops an obsession with more macabre aspects of life or history: whilst this may be a 'passing phase', it could be an indication of a greater concern. Schools should not only record this, but also seek to support and understand the change in character.

Build resilience through a growth mindset

Children who experience the most challenging aspects of life, such as family breakdown, bereavement or finding themselves in a place of potential exploitation, will require specialist support through the school's family support services and external agencies, such as Child and Adolescent Mental Health Services (CAMHS). This will, however, represent only the experience of a small percentage of our children. This doesn't mean that the rest won't face situations where they feel trust has broken down, such as the above example about broken friendships. For all of us, an episode or two of broken trust is part of life and we deal with it through our resilience.

Resilience in the face of obstacles and perceptions of failure and the ability to learn from others are features of a growth mindset. To build resilience in the face of challenge is part of life, and a breach of trust is one of those obstacles we face. As adults, we may have developed strategies through our growth mindset, where we are able to improve what we do. For children, we need to be building their strength and independence through positive relationships from the outset of their schooling, remembering that their previous experience may give them different starting points. Forging and promoting those positive relationships comes from how we set up our classrooms and enable the ways in which children learn.

Children can be supported through activities that encourage collaboration and enable them to fulfil different roles within the group. In other words, teach the children how to work in a group, how to work together and how to trust the decisions and opinions of others. If children aren't taught how to work in a group, they cannot and will not do so effectively. Just as a team game requires coaching in the role each team member plays, so it is in the classroom. Such collaboration allows for mistakes to be built into an activity, and a 'celebration' of the mistake as a learning opportunity is a powerful classroom tool.

Resilience can help children when they feel overwhelmed, something that can be heightened when they feel that the trust of a peer or teacher has been lost. Think for a moment of the impact on a child of being laughed at for their score in a test, or called a name by a friend. Consider also how that child feels if the teacher announces the scores aloud and the anxiety they feel about waiting their turn, knowing that a mocking comment, smirk or giggle might follow. A one-off lower score in a test might be an indication of a lack of understanding, but the child who regularly doesn't achieve a higher score may be facing the double challenge of finding the learning difficult and the negative anticipation of the reaction of their peers. Classroom culture is therefore an important starting point in supporting a growth mindset mentality.

Coping strategies, alongside this positive culture, can be taught generally through whole-class activities. Many children find mindful activities useful, but just as with teacher wellbeing, it is not a solution for everyone. Nevertheless, activities such as deep breathing, mindful laughter and thinking of or finding a safe place are useful calming techniques for many children. Some open and honest discussion about emotions and how situations make children feel has a place in our classroom. Likewise, what anxiety is and how it impacts all of us physically as well as emotionally are useful topics through the primary school and are something we should keep active through to the end of Year 6. The children who will find the transition to Year 7 the easiest are arguably the ones who have had coping strategies modelled, shared and encouraged in their primary setting.

The teaching of growth mindset strategies indicates to the children that their teachers trust them and that they know that mistakes in learning and behaviour can be taken as points for improvement and not for criticism. Feedback that is constructive, not simply full of praise and empty of question and challenge, is the most helpful. Praise in itself isn't what primary teaching looks like; challenging and questioning are fundamental. The skill of the teacher is in developing the language of challenge to keep the trust of the children and to model this language in the ways in which the children interact with each other:

- 'What do you think?'
- 'How can we prove whether it is true or not?'
- 'What might this lead to?'

These and other similarly demanding questions embrace a positive culture in the classroom, show there is challenge and acknowledge that improvement is a personal and an academic expectation for everyone.

Trust within the National Curriculum

Trust has no specific place within the National Curriculum. However, through carefully thought-out planning, considering the widest breadth of curriculum coverage, teachers can identify the opportunity to show how trust, or the lack of it, has contributed to key episodes in British and world history. Religious education is another obvious starting point to include elements of trust and respect, particularly when discussing moral and spiritual issues. In covering the English curriculum, there are no end of relevant books that will cover the development of trust in the relationships between the protagonists and the people they encounter.

Suggested learning opportunities and activities for building trust

Teachers who responded to my survey felt that trust could be covered through a range of activities, including stories that modelled trusting situations and games in PE where trust is an essential element. They also acknowledged the importance of safe spaces, safe means to share their concerns, and the embedding of trust within daily practice through the way in which children share, help and listen.

> *'Children need a safe place and to feel like they're entitled to feelings. Once they feel safe around you, mechanisms need to be in place where they can share in a non-threatening way.'*

Have a good look around your site. Where could these physical safe spaces be? Maybe there is a quiet corner or the shade of a tree where children could go to talk with a friend. Are there spaces where they feel unsafe, out of sight of a supervising adult? Don't forget that the 'space' could be a trusted person, so knowing where that person might be found at given times is also good wellbeing practice.

EYFS	• Begin by teaching the children the traditional topic of people who help us. Ensure that within this is an element of how they help us and why they help us, for example police officers, paramedics, ambulance crew and the fire service. • Use role play to establish that these are safe people to trust and how they might be trusted. • It is important to start from a positive perspective with the youngest children, but also essential to build in the fact that children should always ensure they are with a known and trusted adult. This is crucial to the building of genuine trust as the children get older.
KS1	• Start being specific for this age group about learning to build trust because at this age children potentially start saying things that may be inappropriate in the class about their family and personal circumstances. However, from a safeguarding point of view, it is essential that the children know who and how to tell if they have a problem or worry. • Start to teach who we can tell things to: teacher, teaching assistant, doctor or police officer. • Also begin to cover inadvertently sharing information with somebody we cannot yet trust. This is an ideal time to introduce e-safety and why it's important not to share personal information.
LKS2	• Use PE lessons to show how trust works. Try blindfold games, where one partner leads the other through a path, directs them to hitting a target or runs a race alongside as a guide. • In safe circumstances, falling back to be caught (by an adult) is a trust-based activity that allows children to address their fears and, when complete, to show appreciation for trust.
UKS2	• Building from the falling backwards activity above, the trust built and earned may be very useful if the children go on a school trip, where activities such as abseiling or crate-stacking require trust in both adults and peers.

An assembly about trust

Preparation

Gather some pots of plants (real or sustainable fakes, depending on availability and the amount of mess you are prepared to see; floor covering might be essential). Create a sign saying, 'Gardening help wanted: generous pay for a good job.' Coach four children to act out what follows. This assembly will need two children who are the main protagonists, a child in role as the owner of the property where the sign is and another as grandpa/grandma.

Assembly music

'That's What Friends Are For' by Dionne Warwick, featuring Stevie Wonder and Gladys Knight.

Setting the scene

Have the children in role as the main protagonists play out the following scene: *(The children are walking past the property when they notice the sign.)*

Child 1: Look at this! There's some money for not much work. We can put the money towards some new trainers.

Child 2: Gardening. What do you know about gardening? Your grandpa/grandma does it all.

Child 1: It can't be hard. Trust me.

Freeze the action there. What is the key word the children have used? Establish through questioning that it is 'trust'. Now ask the children to continue (the children playing the owner and grandpa/grandma will also join these next scenes):

Child 1: We saw your sign and would love to help.

Owner: Thank you. I need you to take out all the weeds from my garden. I have an important visitor coming and I don't have the time to do it myself. I want to give them a good impression of the garden. £10 each if you do a good job.

Child 2: That's very kind, thank you.

Child 1: Trust us. We will do a good job.

(The children proceed to do the gardening, with Child 1 in charge, and in the process remove every plant.)

Owner: What have you done? My garden is ruined.

Child 2: I thought you knew what you were doing.

Owner: I'll be telling someone about this.

(At this point grandpa/grandma is walking past.)

Grandpa/grandma: Now what is going on here then?

Child 1: I just copied what you did in your garden. But now it is ruined.

Grandpa/grandma: Ah! That's because I was starting a new flower bed. Everything there was weeds, but here there are some lovely plants. Lucky I am here, because we can save these!

(Everyone joins in to replant everything and the money is handed over.)

Child 1: You deserve this!

(Child 1 hands the money to grandpa/grandma.)

Reflection

- Why is it so difficult for some people to trust others?
- Why is it important for us to trust people?

When children are younger, they find it easy to trust others, but sometimes we find out that we can't trust someone because something goes wrong. We can make trust break down but we can also build it up.

In our story, there could have been a bad experience because trust went wrong. One child could have badly let down the other. Often, we learn not to trust someone as a result of a bad experience.

Trust has to be earned and it is the basis of every relationship that we have. As we trust someone more, the relationship deepens, we become closer friends and we let that person into areas of our life that we might not if we didn't trust them in the same way. That is how permanent, committed relationships are made and kept, often for many years.

- How do you know if you are a trustworthy person?

We need to be sensible when we are deciding whom to trust. Would you give a two-year-old something precious and trust them not to break it? Probably not: the child might break it because they don't yet understand the value of something precious. Would you expect your friend not to break something precious? Most of us probably would trust our friend because they are older and more likely to take care of something that is precious to us.

When we think about trusting someone, we think about whether they actually care for us, whether they have been trustworthy in the past and how they treat other people. Trust needs to be earned and if we let people down, they won't trust us and won't ask us to join in with their activities.

Follow-up

Ask each class to devise their own list of the people they trust as part of their PSHE activities. This can then reflect upon their levels of independence and activity outside of school.

Ask them all for something they could do in school to show their trust, perhaps something that isn't currently permitted: litter-picking, leading play in the Key Stage 1 playground or setting up their own lunchtime activity club. Allow them to negotiate with the headteacher and set the conditions to show they can be trusted.

Success criteria: What does a school that prioritises trust and resilience look like?

- Trust is embedded in the school culture and this enables you to have more powerful conversations to help everyone grow and improve.
- The school invests time and gives structure to trust-building spaces, such as recognising and supporting others.
- Trust is embedded soundly and is an everyday feature of the school. It is encompassed within everything in the school culture: teaching and learning, welfare and safeguarding, lunchtimes and breaktimes.
- Children are trusted to show that they have a growth mindset, that they wish to achieve, improve and develop, and that they understand this as a character goal as much as an academic one.

PART 3

Putting wellbeing values into action

10 Representation and leadership

Chapter overview

Chapter 10 raises the issue of enabling our pupils to experience leadership roles in the primary school, and will argue that not only is equality of opportunity crucial, but that any child should have the opportunity to lead, as this encourages good character development and can support their self-confidence.

Areas discussed

Learning opportunities and activities

Assembly theme

Only some children will have the opportunity to be selected as class ambassadors or as school councillors. Are these always the 'popular' children, the ones who repeatedly seem to be chosen by their peers and by the adults in school to fulfil certain roles? Are these the children who are seen as 'reliable' and 'safe' in case an inspector calls or who will say the right things to the headteacher on a learning walk? We have 30 children in a typical primary classroom; if we rely on the same half a dozen or so, how does that leave the rest feeling?

Leadership roles for children in the primary school could easily fall into the 'give the responsibility to Year 6' category. Whilst it is true that traditional roles such as head boy and girl, prefects and librarians may be given to our older children, couldn't any child potentially take on a leadership role?

The power of pupil voice

Before examining the roles children could undertake to develop leadership skills, consideration should be given to pupil voice, as the way this voice is encouraged and grown in the school environment is part of our school culture and the relationships that we wish to see thrive. Children need to express their thoughts, opinions and experiences in ways that will enable them to be nurtured as trusted friends and reliable members of society – this outcome of pupil voice is equally as important as developing them into potential leaders.

Pupil voice plays an important part in inspection and monitoring, but in the teaching of character, it's essential to give strength and influence to that voice in allowing the children to participate and contribute in a school context. The school council is one means of doing so, but given that only a limited number of children can take part at any one time, the range of roles we give can allow their voice to be heard. 'Voice', so far as wellbeing and character are concerned, need not be the spoken voice, but can be demonstrated as much through actions, as some of the more practical roles discussed below will demonstrate.

School councils and pupil parliaments

The council, or parliament as it is called in some schools, represents a channel for children to discuss matters that actually impact them, from the running of the school library to dealing with issues arising on the playground. There is no fixed structure for a school council, and the size of the school will be a deciding factor in the number of participants and the scope of the elected body. Of greater importance is not the size of the council, but its effectiveness.

To be effective, the council must be representative of the views of all the pupils. The least vocal pupils must be given opportunities to have a 'voice'. Whilst many councils will be chaired by the older pupils, which may be the head girl and boy, the structure needs to allow the youngest members of the group to contribute fully. Having a non-voting adult alongside each key stage can encourage the younger ones to contribute and guide the older children in including everyone.

By having a fallback to class circle times, class councils or a suggestions box, ideas can be fed into the main school council.

Ultimately, school councils are about democracy and are the closest experience children are likely to have of the electoral process that adults experience. In September, if we ask for volunteers for roles on the council, the likelihood is that the most confident children will put themselves forward. Are the most confident children the ones who may make the most of this role? A strategy I have found effective is to ask Year 6 children to nominate another child whom they feel will represent them effectively and empathetically. This often produces results that surprise the children, with children who are naturally more reserved or less confident academically being nominated. Asking their peers why they were chosen often elicits responses linked to core values of character: they listen, have patience or act responsibly. Their subsequent election to the head roles shows the power of the pupil voice and demonstrates that such an election doesn't serve as a popularity contest.

However the council or parliament is chosen, to be effective, meetings should be conducted with serious roles given and sound structures in place. Meetings can be dull for children but create a sense of purpose, and they can feel something is being achieved. Here are some further tips for running a school council:

- Have a facilitator to chair each meeting. Modelled by the adults, this role could rotate and doesn't have to be held by the older children. Sometimes meetings can get out of hand, with either too many people trying to speak, no one speaking at all or a discussion that is missing the point. A facilitator is a person who can ensure that everyone gets their fair say and the meeting sticks to the agenda.
- Use an agenda to keep everyone on topic and as a way of gauging how much and what is being achieved within the time scale available.
- Take minutes. Avoid starting a meeting with no one remembering the exact contents of the last one. Minutes avoid arguments over such details and are a record of any progress made.
- Use voting – when children can't agree on an issue, the chair may decide to hold a vote. This may be a secret ballot or show of hands.
- Exercise patience: this virtue and value is given the chance to thrive in a well-run council. It will teach that success isn't instant and that it requires preparation and effort as well as organisation to be achieved. There may not be a lot achieved initially, but having the framework in place for the future is an essential foundation.

- Forge links with other organisations in order to access information, have some influence and achieve change. Looking at how other organisations operate will be useful, and may even be a good source of funding. Local councils, magistrates, youth forums and Rotary clubs are good starting points, as are bodies within the school community, such as the parent–teacher association, governors and the senior leadership team.

Keeping a regular turnover of children as each year passes can also ensure a balance of involvement over time. By limiting the children to a one-year term of service, until they reach Year 6, over one third of a typical class can have the opportunity to represent their peers, if a model of two children per class is followed. Many primary schools also use a model of one girl and one boy per class to ensure gender balance; if school leaders feel there is a well-established culture of fairness and representation, then the approach of allowing for any two children to be chosen on merit rather than any other criteria can be pursued.

Digital leaders

There are a number of ways in which children can be engaged in a leadership experience. Appointing digital leaders is an effective method of providing leadership experience, whilst at the same time being of assistance to our colleagues. One responsibility of the digital leaders can be the seemingly mundane but essential role of helping younger children to log on to the computers safely; every Reception teacher will breathe a sigh of relief at this service being available. Taking responsibility for attaching laptops to the charging point at the end of the day again is a teacher time-saver and another key job in the efficient running of a computer network, as any teacher who has received an email about leaving resources out in class will attest to.

Depth of significance in this role could come from giving those children an active responsibility in teaching matters of e-safety to younger children, which might mean more coming from a school-age child than it would do from an adult, especially given that the child might be more familiar with a particular application or program that is being used. After training, these children should also be able to provide feedback to teachers about matters such as confidence on the computer and e-safety issues that they have seen arise.

The message about safe internet usage might also be more powerfully delivered from a peer than from an adult. It is possible that a child may discuss an online worry with a classmate rather than with an adult. As teachers, or as teaching assistants, we may inadvertently cause some distress to our children as we discuss how internet history and monitoring work. Our children need to know that internet searches are recorded, mainly for statistical reasons; we mustn't worry the living daylights out of them because they were dared by a friend to type a swear word into a search engine to see what resulted. Responsible usage of the internet could arguably be encouraged by digital leaders acting as peer mentors to encourage the use of safe searching through sites such as Kiddle, which prevent children being exposed to more unscrupulous users of technology.

If schools are thinking not only about teacher workload, but also about promoting independence and responsibility for their pupils, the digital leader role also allows for children to identify broken equipment, detect malfunctioning applications and help teachers who are less confident in teaching computing in understanding trickier concepts such as coding. To raise their profile further, the digital leaders could also provide regular updates as part of a blog on the school website or support the computing lead teacher in a termly email bulletin on e-safety matters.

Suitable and appropriate training, which could just as easily form part of class lessons, as much as specific small-group training, can give children a level of confidence to share their skills in information technology, which after all might be better developed than those of many of the adults in the school.

Children are much more IT-savvy than we often give them credit for, and though they sometimes engage with sites and games that are not appropriate for their age, their experience of them and reaction to what they see could be highly informative for a school in keeping everyone safe. Feedback to teachers on sites that children have found helpful for learning and gaming (because games aren't all bad), as well as those known for scamming and being open to potential cyberbullies, can help teachers to set effective guidelines for the class, which will provide a measure of protection. This is not to suggest that we abrogate responsibility for e-safety, but to recognise that children are better informed about games than we are as adults. How many of our staff meetings have included children teaching staff to use some sites? With the increased reliance on remote learning during the pandemic, this might be an option schools wish to seriously consider.

We can also allow our digital leaders to make presentations to parents and governors, at parents' evenings or during governor visits to school. This gives ownership of the role to children and also allows them to practise and develop their communication skills, both verbal and through the written word.

Sports leaders

Children who are naturally talented athletes, the ones who are often the first pick for teams in PE lessons, are stereotypically chosen as sports leaders. However, give some consideration to those children who aren't picked. Put the emphasis on the word 'leader' rather than 'sports'. Some of our most talented sports coaches and managers were never especially gifted in the field in which they later led – Arsène Wenger, for example, had an insignificant professional career but as a leader was outstanding. As captains, coaches and managers, they are able to use a mix of people skills and motivation to be a driver of sporting success. It is important to teach that sport has winners but it is of greater importance, arguably, that sport also has those who do not 'succeed' in any traditional sense. I very deliberately do not use the word 'loser' because sadly this has very negative connotations and is often used as a playground insult. Knowing how to win with grace and charm sits alongside the skill that enables children to score goals, hit runs, throw further and move faster than others. We must establish the importance of knowing how to lose with dignity and respect for our opponents, for the rules of the game and for fairness.

By giving such roles of leadership to the children who might not normally have such a position, we demonstrate that not only are we an inclusive organisation, but the traditional Corinthian values of fair play, playing to the rules and being a good sport are held in greater value and regard than the simple lifting of trophies and award of medals.

The sports captains could be made responsible for running and organising additional activities at lunch and breaktimes, either with a competitive edge or with an emphasis on fitness or team play. They can act as role models to other children in demonstrating team spirit and good sporting behaviour, including: being courteous to teammates, the referee and the other team; modelling how to be calm and respectful; and thinking about how they can improve their performance the next time, rather than getting cross about an insignificant mistake or how much of the ball crossed a line. Keeping score, setting an example and being responsible for the safe storage of equipment all show excellent traits of good character.

Playground buddies and peer mediators

These roles may be one and the same, or may be separate, but both require a degree of training. In the case of peer mediators, this training should be run by an outside provider, as a degree of skill is required. This could also fit with the principles of restorative justice, which might be employed as part of the school's behaviour management strategy.

In a playground buddy scheme, children from perhaps Year 4 and above can apply to be a buddy to the children in EYFS and Key Stage 1 during lunchtimes. Filling in an application form for the job stating their qualities and why they think they would be suitable requires the older children to think why they would want to perform this role, beyond it being for status. The aim of any such scheme should be to encourage children to be good role models and it can play an important part in creating a safe, friendly, happy and peaceful atmosphere for children during lunchtime. It also gives them some feeling of responsibility. Not only do they help to make the playground a happy place for all the children, but they also offer great help to the staff on duty at lunch.

The role of playground buddies could be:

- to help children to play cooperatively with each other
- to teach children to play a wider range of games and to teach the importance of agreeing to and abiding by rules
- to help more solitary children to make more friends
- to be available as a friend to all the other children.

Peer mediation is conflict resolution for young people by young people. Peer mediators are trained in the process and the skills needed to mediate between two parties neutrally; they are trained to see both sides of an argument and help others to come to a solution themselves. Role play is used and helps the children to find solutions to conflict. When asked, children think they can perhaps understand other children's problems better than adults. The aim of peer mediation should be to encourage pupils to resolve conflict on the school playground using mediation. Conflict is defined as a disagreement, argument or misunderstanding resulting in some kind of falling out. This important role can be extremely beneficial to the children on the playground as well as the peer mediators themselves, as mediation is a core facet of leadership.

Peer mediation is effective when:

- children won't let another play as part of a game or as a group
- unpleasant words have been exchanged
- rude gestures such as pulling faces or blowing raspberries have taken place.

Peer mediation should not be used when:

- any case of fighting has occurred, including play fighting
- there is any physical violence (a child is hit, punched or kicked)
- a child is being called names because of their size, looks, race, religion, gender or perceived sexual preference
- a child is being coerced to do something that they know is wrong.

In these instances, an adult will always intervene as these are essentially safeguarding matters. The training your mediators receive should help them to identify such incidents and call for them to ask an adult to deal with the situation.

Environmental leaders

As covered in Chapter 4, children are motivated by issues in regard to the environment, in protecting it and keeping it safe and useable. Many teachers would appreciate the help offered by children who wish to volunteer to keep things tidy, but the availability of this opportunity allows children to develop another aspect of leadership aside from the more 'popular' role of head boy and head girl. This is also a way to enable younger children to take on a leadership role and to encourage them to challenge adults in appropriate ways about their environmental awareness: there is nothing more awkward for a Year 6 child (or teacher for that matter) than being told off by a seven-year-old for putting plastic in the recycled paper bin!

Other roles for our eco-leaders include:

- litter-picking and sorting into appropriate bins (this will need training and suitable equipment: gloves and litter-pickers; **warning:** know your site, as broken bottles and drugs paraphernalia may often be disposed of on some school grounds)
- collecting the recycling
- closing doors and turning off lights in unattended classrooms at break and lunchtimes
- preparing graphs and reports relating to how classes are reducing, reusing and recycling
- preparing assemblies, parental presentations and newsletters on their current work, aims and ambitions.

Children acting as ambassadors for the principles included in Chapter 4 gives a robust message that environmental awareness is embedded in the school culture.

Healthy eating ambassadors

Working closely with the healthy schools lead, these children can help in conducting healthy lunch audits. The potential impact of children leading in this role on their peers' lunch choices, particularly in packed lunches, might be greater than any impact an adult might have. When teachers and school leaders question parents about 'unhealthy' packed lunch options, there can sometimes be a backlash as parents might consider they are being unfairly judged for the food they provide; if the message comes from the findings of our young leaders, it might attract more attention.

The healthy eating ambassadors could design an ideal healthy packed lunch. This could be supported through activities such as searching the online prices of items on the website of the local supermarkets, calculating the cost of a basket and perhaps leading a workshop for other children, demonstrating how easily and inexpensively a healthy lunch can be put together.

Junior road safety officers

Local authority websites have a wealth of information to support this crucial role, which supports the principles laid out in Chapter 5. Junior road safety officers (JRSOs) can help the adult responsible for road safety, and also work with the local road safety officer – though not all areas have them – to promote road safety issues within the school and the local community. An ongoing role, throughout the year the JRSOs could be involved in a range of activities, including:

- maintaining a notice board or part of the school website and making sure the road safety information is up to date
- talking in an assembly or leading activities in class on road safety themes
- working with younger children in road safety role play situations
- arranging competitions and promotions on themes such as being safe and being seen, or scooter and cycle safety
- promoting campaigns such as walking to school weeks or months, collecting and collating data and awarding certificates
- taking part in the appointment of their successors.

Classroom monitors

Children serving in roles such as milk monitor or being in charge of sharpening the pencils will be familiar to all of us from our own primary school days. As primary teachers, employing our classroom monitors in an era when our time is finite enables us to keep our classrooms tidy and have a clutter-free learning environment. However, having an established list of responsibilities is also an opportunity to promote the principle that any child can be a leader. By transforming this list to a rota, in the course of one year, every child can have responsibility for each aspect of the class, from the mundane to the 'prestigious'. What, on the surface, might appear to be a simple part of classroom organisation is, in fact, one means of delivering a part of character education in endorsing equality of opportunity and a culture of teamwork and togetherness amongst the class.

Leadership within the National Curriculum

The word 'leadership' does not appear in the National Curriculum. What do appear, though, are opportunities, particularly through history, to discuss the lives and impacts of leaders and, through the English curriculum, to read and write about them.

Political leaders and campaigners make a good starting point, particularly leaders representing the range of cultures and faiths in our communities. Most primary children will have had some lessons about Nelson Mandela, but surely there is also a place to learn about Kwame Nkrumah. It is important to know about Mahatma Gandhi, but equally to learn about the lives of Muhammad Ali Jinnah and Jawaharlal Nehru. For every lesson about Martin Luther King, there needs to be one on Rosa Parks, who did much more than simply take a seat on a bus. We need not limit our study to the expired: Kamala Harris, Michelle Obama, Sadiq Khan and Nicola Sturgeon all set examples, and make mistakes, that merit coverage.

Local leadership also provides a wealth of opportunity. A good local MP will respond to children's letters and may visit. Mayors, councillors and magistrates can give their time to discuss civic responsibilities, whilst the fire, ambulance and police services demonstrate leadership skills through the principle of safeguarding their community.

Suggested learning opportunities and activities for developing leadership skills

Children will see their class teachers and senior staff as the leaders they aspire to be. They may also see good modelling of leadership skills from members of their family, from parents, grandparents or siblings, but equally they may not have this example from home. What we set as an exemplar of what leadership skills may look like will have a huge influence over young minds, but we need to be acutely aware that societal norms may not be celebrated in the same way in the children's home environment. Today's children are tomorrow's leaders, and whilst leadership skills can come naturally to some, other children will learn lessons along the way that significantly impact them later in life. The right words and actions at the right time can make all the difference. The greatest impact teachers can have on their children as leaders is to set the best example, by word, by deed and by accountability.

EYFS	• Encourage team and group activities from the outset to show that every child has a valuable part to play in the culture of the school. • Invite outside visitors from groups such as Rainbows and Beavers, organisations that develop leadership skills in their own ways and which also help to promote community cohesion. • Promote confident communication with adults. From the outset, particularly in role play areas, encourage speaking in full sentences and modelling this for children whose language isn't as well developed as others.
KS1	• When a child works on a task, it can be tempting to jump in and help, especially a child who is seen to be struggling. Instead, consider stepping back and letting the pupil work through it themselves and develop a degree of resilience. Afterwards, review the obstacles and challenges that emerged during the task and ask for ideas on how things could have been done differently.

	• Outside visitors could include local sports clubs, particularly those promoting equality of opportunity: rugby and football for girls in particular. • Build negotiation skills. Every good leader knows the art of compromise. Instead of giving the children a firm 'yes' or 'no' to a request, make an offer and allow them to counter that offer by offering solid points. Teach them negotiation skills like never giving something up without asking for something else in return. • Build decision-making skills too. Rather than overwhelming children with too many options, weighing the benefits and deficits of two choices – for instance, 'Shall we have our art lesson inside or outside this afternoon?' – gives a meaningful context to the decision-making process. • Build in the opportunity to make mistakes and to learn from them. Teach that it is better to be wrong and know why something is wrong, than to be correct but not know how or why the answer is correct.
LKS2	• Begin to train children as mentors and mediators. Trusted friends and classmates can play an invaluable role as mentors, providing children with another layer of trust after their class teacher and teaching assistant. • Use vision boards. A way to teach children goal-setting is through the use of vision boards, which is more than a cut and paste activity, but a process in which they can be taught how to visualise what they want to achieve. • Emphasise perseverance. The best leaders learn to handle failure as gracefully as they handle success. It's important to expose future leaders to disappointment rather than protecting them from it. Children need to learn how to accept defeat not as failure but as an opportunity to move forward. • Show trust in your mentors and mediators by rewarding them appropriately for their work, but also give recognition to those they have mediated between, recognising positive changes in conduct as a result of the peer mentoring process.

UKS2	• Investigate the lives of great leaders and organise a 'general election' for the best, with groups of children 'campaigning' on their behalf. Whether the vote is in the class, year group or across the school, this gives audience and purpose to the children's writing and communication skills and allows children to take ownership of their role models. • Encourage volunteering and entrepreneurial activities. Running a stall to sell healthy snacks or excess stock of old books to parents after school allows older children to exercise their communication and negotiation skills. • Attend the school residential trip. At whichever point in the school year this occurs, either as a team-building activity at the beginning of Year 6 or a bonding exercise at the end of the year, the residential visit is filled with opportunities to participate in group activities. Working as a team in building the most robust raft, encouraging the child who has sat for ten minutes at the top of the abseiling tower or using previously taught but most likely unused navigation skills around an unfamiliar location – all allow for leadership to be demonstrated, perhaps by the children we and their peers might least expect. • Teach planning skills. Make this practical, such as planning for an end-of-term picnic or the post-SATs visit to a theme park. Giving children responsibility for finding prices, planning a schedule or organising menus gives them an idea of distributive leadership and of making decisions that are financially and time efficient. • In small ways, today's leaders can prepare younger generations for their future as business leaders. Each of these suggestions will not only create better leaders, but can also help children to perform better in school and develop better personal relationships throughout life. • Ask the children to write about their role models and why they believe them to be exemplary in their conduct. By thinking about what their role models do beyond their normal role, such as Marcus Rashford and his campaign relating to food poverty, we can encourage the children to think beyond mere celebrity, which can be quite a shallow concept.

A leadership assembly

What might it be like to be prime minister for a day?

This assembly, although designed with a light-hearted approach in mind, looks at the serious notion of prioritising and decision-making.

Think about the age of the children in the assembly. If speaking to older children, the decisions could be more challenging, generating more thoughtful contributions; with the whole primary age range, the issues raised could be more immediate to the experience of the younger children.

Preparation

Prepare cards (A3 or A2 sized) and slides showing a number of 'problems' to be solved. By making these issues something relevant to the school, such as having additional homework, adding or removing something from school dinners, children having some additional playtime equipment or a change to the school uniform, we can add some relevance to the impact of this assembly.

Arrange a 'dispatch box' to speak from at the front of the hall, flanked by two rows of benches to resemble parliamentary benches.

A few days before the assembly, select one child to be the 'prime minister' and a group of six to eight children to be members of parliament (MPs). Split the MPs into two opposing parties. Give each of the MPs one of the cards with the 'problems' and ask them to prepare a short speech about the problem and why they think it needs to be dealt with urgently. A child in the opposing party should prepare a counter argument. Make sure you rehearse the debates with the children ahead of the assembly.

Assembly music

'What's Going On?' by Marvin Gaye will set an appropriate tone here.

Setting the scene

Explain to the children that one of them is going to be prime minister for the day. The prime minister will face a range of problems to deal with in 'parliament' and has to place these in the order in which they want to deal with them.

Also explain that there are going to be several people who believe their problem is more important than everyone else's. The prime minister's task is going to be to listen and to make decisions that are best for everyone.

As the cards and slides are shown, each of the children on the benches presents their problem to the class or assembly. The 'opposition' bench provides a counter argument.

If you have children with sufficient levels of responsibility and confidence, either as your prime minister or as your MPs, they can add a level of questioning and challenge into the discussion. Having a 'prime minister' stood at the 'dispatch box' will increase the sense of reality if the children have seen such images on the television.

Reflection

- How difficult was each decision?
- Was the prime minister trying to please people?
- How will we know whether the decision made is the correct one?

Follow-up

- Ask the children on the school council to debate and reach a decision on one of the issues raised in the assembly, preferably one that will have a concrete resolution once taken to the headteacher, governors or school caterers, depending on the matter chosen.
- Encourage the school council to find a way to communicate the result of their work to children and parents: via a parent email, a parent communication app or an announcement in assembly. Show them what the power of reasonably argued discussion and genuinely robust leadership can do.
- Keep the decision in high profile through display, discussions about its effectiveness, feedback on improvement and through adults (including governors) showing a genuine interest in the outcome of it.

Success criteria: What does a school that prioritises pupil leadership look like?

- The school ethos supports a genuine equality of opportunity for children to shine as leaders. Are your young leaders the children who always seem to have these roles or do the quieter and more reserved children have the opportunity as well?
- The decisions and actions the children take in their roles are respected by the community and are supported and promoted by the adults in school.
- The roles given to the children have a purpose. Children receive feedback from adults and from peers. They are also rewarded and acknowledged for the roles they fulfil.
- Learning from mistakes is built into the leadership roles as part of developing resilience and can be returned to as part of an ongoing discussion about all children aspiring to be the best that they can be.

11 Respect for diversity: equality and equity

Chapter overview

This chapter will discuss ways in which we could cover diversity within the context of wellbeing and character. Diversity in itself would fill several volumes, but within these pages I hope to discuss some key issues.

The events of summer 2020, namely the death of George Floyd and the associated surge of support for Black Lives Matter, have ensured that diversity is very much on the national and global agenda. That it took a tragedy such as this to draw attention to the issues around respect for diversity disguises the fact that, as teachers, we have been aware of and have supported the interests of a diverse community for a substantial period of time. When we teach diversity with children, we need to think about matters of race and faith but also consider attitudes and challenges around gender equality, sexism, sexuality and disability. The skills and knowledge that we provide our children with in celebrating diversity will be a true test of character and of how well they are prepared to look after each other and the wider community.

Equality or equity?

In order to address the teaching of diversity, teachers need to know the difference between the terms equality and equity. Equality means that everyone is the same, is treated in the same way and has the same rights, status and privileges. In teaching equity, however, we need to acknowledge the different starting points that exist and that the difference in circumstances requires support in order to be able to reach a position of equality. This is an essential part of vocabulary knowledge for teachers and children to understand. Though both promote fairness, equality and equity need to be considered together. There is an image of three children of different heights watching a baseball game over a fence. The image for 'equality' shows all three standing on a single box, the taller child with a clear view, the middle one with his head just over the fence and the smaller one standing on the box but left looking through a hole in the fence. In the contrasting image for 'equity', the boxes are redistributed, the taller child giving up their box, as they were able to see over the fence without it, the middle child keeping one box, and the smaller child standing on two boxes and now able to see as clearly as the others.

We work from a position of equity as dedicated teachers. Children who find difficulty in accessing aspects of the curriculum are supported through specific resources, adult support, differentiated tasks and additional time. The professional language we use in discussing children is also reflective of our understanding and practice of equity; instead of using a judgemental and cover-all term such as 'autistic', it is increasingly preferable to use the term 'neurodiverse' and 'neurotypical' in our discourse.

The consideration of our language in how we talk about diversity plays an important role in how we model to children the expectations that we have of them. With disability, as Elizabeth Wright sets out in the piece later in this chapter on page 172, terms like 'overcome' and 'suffering' aren't helpful or appropriate. Much of the discriminatory language around diversity tends to label people as different and think of disadvantage over advantage, creating more barriers to equity through lack of knowledge. There is also the case that some language might represent a 'microaggression', which is a verbal indignity, sometimes intentional as a provocation, sometimes not through lack of knowledge.

The language we teach in regard to diversity needs to include the terms racism, sexism, homophobia, ableism and disablism as well as the words prejudice and discrimination. We need to be specific, because if we are not, the chances to eradicate such language and behaviour will be limited.

Race and ethnicity

When schools returned in September 2020, many of them will have had in place lessons that directly supported and promoted racial diversity. In our school, we called this 'The Colours of Us' and we celebrated the diverse ethnic and cultural backgrounds of our families. As a word of caution, although it was very important that this was covered, it was equally essential that this was not a mere token but something that was embedded within teaching and in the broader way in which children interacted with each other and with adults in the community. When we see criticism of teaching about diversity and comments suggesting we should be teaching that 'all lives matter', these neglect to notice that our primary history curriculum is very 'white' and almost entirely English – as opposed to British – and doesn't cover topics such as the impact of colonial expansionism and the slave trade. It is the slaves transported to the 13 colonies who are the direct ancestors of many African-American and Black British people; our nation's history directly impacted upon inequalities and attitudes three centuries ago that remain and have been exacerbated by the course of history. If we are serious in wanting to make good global citizens of our children, we need to teach them not only what racism is and why it is wrong, but how it originated.

Race and ethnicity are terms that need to be understood by all staff in school and taught specifically to the children. Race usually has a narrow definition, based on biological or physical characteristics, such as skin colour. Ethnicity has a broader definition, drawing from cultural expression and place of origin. Racism is easier to define; it is prejudice and discrimination against the race or ethnicity of others based on social perceptions of the differences between people.

It is in the early years of schooling that attitudes can be embedded, but negative beliefs can originate at home. When we address comments such as 'this is a game only white-skinned children can play', we can discuss this in a circle time session and talk about why it is important to be friends and respect each other. The parent sending a sharply worded email or loudly raising their voice objecting to their child learning about and celebrating other cultures and faiths is another matter altogether. Parents have the right to withdraw their child only from religious education lessons and from the sex education elements of the relationships and sex education (RSE) curriculum, but schools need to take a firm stand against what might be intimidatory behaviour by some parents in regard to other aspects of the curriculum. One example might be questioning a class trip to a mosque or a gurdwara, and then pressuring other parents to challenge the visit, trying to force its cancellation. When a school has a culture that promotes diversity and inclusivity, hopefully the issue will not arise. However, there are places where, fuelled by the uncertain politics of the last two decades, pockets of challenge to our diverse society exist. If we want our children to be respectful of race and ethnicity, the language to challenge prejudice and discrimination needs to be practised.

The decision of the England men's football squad to 'take a knee' before the matches in the delayed European Championship in 2021 provides a strong reminder of why challenging discrimination is so important. Though some commentators have debated the reasoning behind such an action, it is important for children to understand that such a simple act can represent a strong and communal voice against belief and conduct that is wrong.

In March 2021, the Sewell Report, the report of the Commission on Race and Ethnic Disparities, was published. In terms of education, the report pointed to disparity in family, geography and poverty, acknowledging the need to support children of all ethnic and lower socio-economic backgrounds who are not deemed as succeeding. The report recommended greater teacher and governor diversity, building social and cultural capital, teaching an inclusive curriculum, promoting good behaviour and pastoral support, and empowering pupils to make informed choices about their futures as elements of good schools. The statement in the report that Britain is no longer a country where the 'system is deliberately rigged against ethnic minorities' is clearly not shared by all those who read it. The joint response of the main teaching unions made it clear that they felt it diminished the impact of structural and institutional racism in the lives of black people (TUC, 2021). Labour MP David Lammy said the report was an 'insult to anybody and everybody across this country who experiences institutional racism' (ITV News, 2021).

I interviewed Shakira Martin to discuss the Sewell Report and the impact of racism, discrimination, equality and equity in schools, and I am very grateful for her insights, which I have detailed below. Shakira is a former president of the National Union of Students (NUS) 2017–2019, the first president from the further education sector. She is a passionate advocate for the post-16 sector and has campaigned to raise awareness of student poverty. She is a mother of two primary school children.

An interview with Shakira Martin

Do you think schools have a clear idea about what racism, discrimination, equality and equity look like?

I think the main issue is how to build awareness into the curriculum and also recruitment of staff. It is empowering and fruitful to have a diverse staff who can use their insight and experience to help shape decision-making processes. Schools understand what they need to do in terms of equality, but equity and an equitable system are what they need to recognise. Teachers should be trained in this.

It is welcoming that schools are acting on issues relating to race, but in truth racism has been happening for years. Different areas have different issues and the resources and capacity to support and act on this will differ too. This will come at a cost – perhaps there needs to be a 'premium' for this just like the Pupil Premium.

Our perspective of the world affects our pedagogy and the strength of what we embed in our curriculum will be seen in how it plays out culturally. It is important to know about Martin Luther King, Malcolm X, Nelson Mandela – they are legends – but it is important too to know about the people who have stood on their shoulders, who might not be as well known but have played a vital role.

We should also give credit to children who know more about what is going on than some teachers think.

The overarching term BAME doesn't give useful information to schools as there are differences within the Black community. Mental health, for example, wasn't often spoken of in the Black community; there has been a stigma and little culture of resilience. There are signs of movement though in discussing mental health within the Black community.

How does your experience of discrimination in school compare to the experience of your children? Is the Sewell Report a true reflection of racism in the UK?

The Sewell Report is a missed opportunity. It is disrespectful of the lived experiences of discrimination and prejudice of millions across this country.

When I was younger I wasn't aware of structural racism; I just thought life was hard. It was my time in the NUS that made me aware of structural racism and its impact.

Has it changed for the better? No, it has got worse in many ways. Children know it is wrong to use the N word and nipping it in the bud immediately is essential. Institutional racism is a bigger challenge; schools can be institutionally racist from how their systems have been built up and where stereotyping and discrimination aren't challenged.

It is great when you have a Black girl playing Mary in the Nativity but think about the baby Jesus too by using a Black doll. Schools that act appropriately like this are making a step in the right direction, as are those that grant a day off for Eid or other festivals as well as those who have a diverse staff and governing body. Allyship is a welcome commitment; if you do your bit, you are challenging discrimination.

Gender equality

In my first year of teaching, I was observed in one lesson and it was pointed out to me that I had responded more to the boys than to the girls. This surprised me, as I had always felt that I had demonstrated an equal opportunities attitude in class, but having seen the informal tally (60 per cent to 40 per cent), it made me realise that I was responding to the more vocal parts of the class. This taught me that diversity awareness as a teacher should be included within basic class management and to give voice to the quiet ones, which did include a number of the boys, without suppressing the vocal. The observation was a science lesson, and though the outcomes of the lesson and of the year were fair and accurate, this observation stayed with me and made me acutely aware of the power of questioning and how 'differentiated questioning' impacted not only the academic needs of the class but also issues of equality and equity.

Take a moment to reflect here, whether as a reader you are a trainee, class teacher or school leader. Which subjects would you regard as ones where boys would perform better than girls? Mathematics perhaps, or science and maybe design technology? Do you consider that girls perform better in English, particularly in writing, or in music and the other creative subjects? This is not a criticism, but a reflection: does this reflection show attitudes in society, in school or something else? Now actually consider your classes from the past. My highest achievers in Year 6 mathematics have all been girls, three of whom scored 99 per cent on levelled SATs. My best group of Year 6 writers were all boys, solid level 5 achievers. Stereotyping of gender with subjects is not only inaccurate but dismissive of potential. For example, in many schools, the majority, if not all, of the choir is made up of girls. Why is this? It could boil down to attitudes in the community that this isn't something boys do. Equally, it could reflect on attitudes within the school community and be a reflection of peer pressure on boys not to participate. This is the point at which school values should challenge this kind of attitude, not in any aggressive way but in a manner to push the boundaries of the school culture. Look at your school clubs; which lists are more heavily dominated by one gender and how could you restore a balance?

Sport is one area where gender discrimination attitudes linger. In my early years of teaching, given the rather obvious 'only male teacher apart from the head' role of running the football team, I attended my first fixture meeting and innocently asked whether I could pick girls for the school team. This was in 1993, so not ancient history. I was told that if I selected girls for any competitive fixture, my school would be disqualified from all competitions. Unbelievable. This rule was reversed in the next year or so, but when I selected a girl for the team, a letter was sent to the headteacher in protest. In what could have been a perfectly scripted moment, the player in question was sent on as a substitute, scored with her first touch and won the game.

Should we be shocked at this attitude? Even in 2021, there are comments made about female officials and questions about how Alex Scott, a former England international, can be chosen as a pundit on *Match of the Day*. Do you still have 'girls can't play football' attitudes from the boys at school, causing issues at break and lunch? Any teacher wishing to address the issue of gender equality through sport could take as a starting point the story of Lily Parr. See the box on the following page for more information.

Sexuality

In 2019, parental protest objecting to the 'No Outsiders' initiative outside a primary school in Birmingham led to nationwide media coverage (BBC News, 2019). Eventually resulting in an injunction banning demonstrations outside the school, the complaints related to teaching about same-sex relationships and transgender identities. Protests resulted in disruption to lessons, but also included some harmful and untrue allegations. Demonstrations spread to other schools in Birmingham.

The new RSE guidance has a number of themes running through it, the most important being safe, caring and respectful relationships. It recognises that families can look different between different households. There is no promotion

The life of Lily Parr: the greatest female footballer?

During the First World War, women's football became extremely popular and women's teams regularly packed out football league stadiums, with the most popular team being the Dick, Kerr Ladies, representing a factory in the town of Preston. After the war, the team continued to show great success, often raising funds for injured veterans of the war, and in a game against St Helens Ladies, the 14-year-old winger from St Helens caught the eye of the Dick, Kerr Ladies manager. This winger was Lily Parr, and she and her teammate Alice Woods were offered a place on the Dick, Kerr Ladies team and a job in the factory, reportedly for a payment of ten shillings for every game she played, with a supplementary payment of a packet of Woodbine cigarettes!

In her first season, Parr scored 43 goals and it was reported in the local press that there was 'probably no greater football prodigy in the whole country'. Described as having a 'kick like a mule', she allegedly broke a male goalkeeper's arm as he tried to block one of her shots.

Women's football had been tolerated during the war because it raised morale but its continued success post war became a threat to the professional game. On 5 December 1921, the Football Association banned female footballers from playing on professional pitches, commenting that 'the game of football is quite unsuitable for females and ought not to be encouraged'.

Lily and her teammates were potentially denied professional careers because of this ruling, which refused them access to professional facilities. It was not until 1970 that women were allowed to play in the stadiums where we now see them so regularly in the Women's Super League.

Parr played until 1950, retiring at the age of 45. She scored nearly 1,000 goals, her final one in an 11–1 drubbing of Scotland. She lived long enough to see the governing body overturn its previous ruling. In 2008, the Football Association issued an apology for its treatment of women's football in Parr's time.

Lily Parr could very easily be added to any discussion of powerful and influential women, not only in her role as a talented and passionate footballer but also in the fact that she and her partner were open about their relationship, at a time when members of the LGBT+ community were ostracised.

of one kind of relationship; rather, it promotes the characteristics of friendship in the form of trust, respect, kindness and generosity.

In the primary school setting, aside from teaching the content about relationships agreed after consultation with the school community, our most likely dealings with sexuality are going to relate to discriminatory language. Although the word 'gay' has been used as a descriptive for a substantial period of time, its use as a pejorative is what we are likely to encounter most frequently. Children may use the term as an insult to others, and this requires intervention to ensure that the children using this term understand that it is homophobic and why it shouldn't be used. Whether it is a form of bullying or mimicking behaviours seen elsewhere, neither is acceptable and the behaviour policy should be applied appropriately. Again, we return to staff understanding of what homophobic, biphobic and transphobic language is, and how to challenge it.

However, we also need to consider the impact upon the children on the receiving end of this behaviour. Their self-esteem, confidence and developing identity are all potentially impacted, and being on the receiving end of any pejorative term serves only to undermine trust and induce a feeling of rejection. The school with the sound system of values will have support for this scenario in place.

Disability

In my NQT class, many of whom were with me for two years, I taught one young man who was born missing a right arm, with three fingers at a wrist joint formed at his shoulder. He found writing extremely difficult, but he was a remarkably talented artist and his patience, skill and eye for detail earned him much admiration from his peers. He loved the opportunity to take part in sport. Kwik Cricket was ideal, particularly in batting, where only playing with a left arm enabled him to develop an excellent grasp of technique and to impress his friends with some sharp one-handed catching.

The moment that always stood out for me, and one that celebrated him as an individual proudly representing his school, was at the annual swimming gala. Our school never performed particularly strongly and the most we hoped for was a handful of second or third places in a programme of some 30 events. When it was time for our young man's race, there were some unfortunate sniggers and comments from children in the other schools, swiftly dealt with by a few sharp words and hard stares from their teachers. Needless to say, he not only won his race, but finished it with his closest opponent half a length behind. There wasn't a dry eye amongst our team and our supporters.

Giving children with disabilities opportunities in sports isn't as great a challenge as you might imagine. It takes an open mindset and a little imagination with resourcing to enable children in wheelchairs or with limb differences the opportunity to take part, just as much as their peers. There is no reason why a child in a wheelchair shouldn't take part in races on sports day, for example. They can compete in very much equal terms in certain throwing events. The sport of boccia, the only sport specifically developed for the Paralympic movement, is a great leveller. We have included boccia at my school, where it has allowed children in wheelchairs the opportunity to compete alongside their peers and to teach them some specific skills. Like many others, I first heard of boccia at the London 2012 Paralympics. Having seen it in action, it not only allows the opportunity for children to compete on equal terms, but also allows them to celebrate a measure of sporting success and skill that they might not otherwise have the opportunity to show.

Elizabeth Wright is a proud Australian Paralympian, winning silver and bronze medals at the Atlanta and Sydney Paralympics. She now resides in the UK and is a speaker, writer and activist. This piece is edited from one of her blog posts and is included here with her permission.

There is no such thing as 'overcoming' a disability, by Elizabeth Wright

I'd just finished my talk to a room full of high school students and I had asked if anyone had any questions.

'Yes?' I nodded at the young man halfway up the lecture theatre.

He shifted uncomfortably in his seat, glanced at his friend, and then asked, 'How did you overcome your disability?'

Overcome.

The word seemed to reverberate around the room. I could see it echoed in all of the other students' faces. A questioning, a judgement, a curiosity about the story I had just told them.

My body responded the way that it always does when I hear the word 'overcome'. I felt my hackles rise up, my fight response kicking in. As though the word itself is a threat. And then my heart sank. Deeply. I felt disappointed. Disappointed that words and terms such as 'overcome', 'despite', 'even though' and 'in spite of' are still used with such abandon when talking about disability.

'I didn't.'

My response confused the boy. I had just spent 45 minutes talking to the students about how I went from being born with my disability to medalling at the Paralympic Games. To some degree, I did understand why he was confused. And it was my job to help him and his classmates understand why it wasn't OK to link the term 'overcome' with disability.

The Paralympics have been pushed into the spotlight more and more over the years. With this new-found popularity comes a presentation of the athlete as transcendence. The athlete who has 'overcome' the odds.

The most prominent example of this is from the London Paralympics 2012. Channel 4 in the UK pushed the idea of 'superhuman' disabled athletes. Calling someone superhuman within the context of disability implies a level of 'overcoming'. For many disabled people, including some Paralympic athletes, this contributed to harmful stereotypes around disability.

As a Paralympian myself, I can certainly say that I am not superhuman and I haven't overcome my disability to go to the Paralympics. What I did do was recognise the talent I had in my sport and then work my bloody arse off to get there. Just like all athletes, Paralympians and Olympians alike. This is why I stand with other disabled people who fought against the simplistic notion of disabled people as superhuman.

There is a dichotomous disability narrative that plagues disabled people more and more. The common social notion of disability is that of overcoming the weakness in your own body and mind. And social narratives claim Paralympians are those who have 'successfully overcome' their disabilities, and everyone else is either lazy, weak or 'faking it'.

Countless times I have been told that I am 'overcoming' my disability or that I have to 'overcome' my disability. It is as though my disability isn't a part of me or my life experience. It is as though disability is some kind of monster on my back that prevents me from achieving or living a normal life. Even though it is a part of my body, my DNA makeup, people feel they have a right to motivate me to do better, to be better. That through their encouragement and admiration of my doing normal things I have somehow rid myself of disability. That I have somehow 'overcome' it. There is such a reductionist quality about the term 'overcoming'. By reducing disabled people to some kind of ableist miracle fantasy, you are completely eliminating every other aspect of their identity.

We do not exist to be your symbol of hope or optimism.

This performative advice follows a similar script: be positive. Don't give up. Smile. Be polite. Grieve. Accept your disability. Do your best... and finally, ask yourself if you are happy.

The advice implies a censoring of one's behaviour so as to keep non-disabled people comfortable and unchallenged. Disabled people, therefore, can't be angry, grumpy, sad or frustrated. Because if you are any of these things, you are failing to 'overcome' your disability. You are failing to 'overcome' yourself. The point is that there is no 'overcoming' a disability.

Or rather it isn't me who needs to overcome my disability, but the non-disabled people whom I interact with, who design the spaces I live in and who teach, support or employ me. It isn't me who stares at my arm and leg; it isn't me who fails to consider whether I could physically use that space or not; it isn't me who made an assumption about what I could or couldn't do because of my disability. This isn't me overcoming my disability, but questioning those around me: what are you afraid of?

And how can I help *you* overcome my disability?

Diversity in the National Curriculum

There is little, if anything, specific in the words of the National Curriculum documents directly addressing diversity, but I would contend that there is plentiful scope for content that would satisfy both our statutory requirements alongside the children's character and wellbeing development. Many issues around a diverse curriculum can be addressed through powerful and appropriate stories, ideas for which are listed in the Further reading section. Writing, likewise, provides excellent coverage, especially when the children engage in biographical writing. Key Stage 1 history allows for the study of significant figures from the past and Key Stage 2 allows for a look at changes in an aspect of social history in Britain into which any aspect of diversity can fit. Think too about how art, music and design technology can draw upon a rich vein of diverse influences without ever being seen as tokenistic. PE too has a plentiful range for diversity, not only in adaptations for children with different physical needs, but also in embracing games and sports from different cultures.

There is a place in the National Curriculum reserved for spoken language; it is there on the first page of the English section of the document. Though it links spoken language to the development of reading and writing, within the wellbeing and character development of the children, spoken language should be a tool for debate, challenge, reasoning and conciliation, significant tools in a diverse school culture.

Suggested learning opportunities and activities for addressing diversity

Rather than provide specific activities here, I am going to suggest that you consider context and need in planning how to address diversity, because school communities change in their socio-economic profile and in their racial-ethnic diversity as the housing market and the local economy changes. Any teachers who have been at a school for a long period will testify to this.

I will, however, list some general activities that can be tailored to suit your context:

- Listening to and learning songs from different cultures and in different languages.
- Playing games from different cultures. Mancala has always been a favourite of mine.
- Preparing and eating food from your school community and beyond.
- Having open conversations about biases and stereotypes.
- Being clear that asking questions is acceptable.
- Ensuring that the artists and musicians you study, and the visitors you welcome, reflect the diversity you wish to promote.

The diverse school and the diverse classroom have characteristics where language that promotes diversity and challenges prejudice has a high profile during academic learning and through the other parts of the day, playtimes, lunch breaks and assemblies, the times when children socialise, talk and play. Diverse classrooms aren't made solely by displays and books celebrating the distinctive features of the school; they acknowledge diversity equally by classroom organisation, seating plans and how the children talk to and with each other. These classrooms acknowledge who are the quiet voices and give them a chance to be heard.

A curriculum that is diverse can be planned ahead, but also needs capacity to respond at short notice. An incident of racist language, one of sexist attitudes or some other expression of prejudice will need dealing with through behaviour policies, but can also become a learning opportunity that reflects the values of the school and the expectations we have of the children. Language, values and attitudes enable and empower the children to make the correct choices, which will be discussed in the final chapter.

A diversity assembly

A script or outline isn't provided for this assembly. When talking to the children about diversity, discrimination and prejudice, telling the story of important people and how they sought to challenge the barriers in their way provides an excellent starting point for discussion children can follow up in their classes.

By all means tell the stories of Nelson Mandela, Malala Yousafzai, Martin Luther King and Rosa Parks, all inspirational people, but children might be limited to the same diet of subjects repeated several times over. They may also be exposed to some inaccuracies: Rosa Parks was not, for example, the instigator of the bus sit-in, just the best known, with several having taken place before her protest.

Below are a few suggestions, as a starting point, of inspirational people in different areas, whose lives have had an impact on challenging issues relating to race, gender, sexuality or disability:

- **Astronauts:** Sally Ride, Eileen Collins, Helen Sharman, Ronald McNair, Mae C. Jemison, Kalpana Chawla.
- **Scientists:** Marie Curie, Ada Lovelace, Katherine Johnson, Mary Anning, Valerie Thomas, Stephen Hawking.
- **Sports people:** Walter Tull, Ellie Simmonds, Steph Houghton, Sachin Tendulkar, Charlotte Edwards, Tessa Sanderson, Billie Jean King, Justin Fashanu, Sir Vivian Richards, Nicola Adams.
- **Politicians:** Baroness Floella Benjamin, Oona King, Joanne Anderson, Leo Varadkar, Jacinda Ardern, Franklin and Eleanor Roosevelt.

- **Artists and entertainers:** Frida Kahlo, Ravi Shankar, Ai Weiwei, Josephine Baker, Oprah Winfrey, Olly Alexander, Andrea Bocelli.

This is by no means an exhaustive list. Think about your school context and the themes you wish to address.

Follow-up

If this assembly was being led as part of a school focus on diversity, classes could take one person each and look further at their work, inspiration, lessons from their life and how they are a particular role model. A display and a further assembly led by the children would be a natural progression from the initial assembly. Please be wary of not letting this become a box-ticking exercise, but ensure the language used is built into the daily discourse in the school.

Success criteria: What does a school that prioritises diversity look like?

- The language that promotes and protects diversity is prominent in the school; it goes beyond the website and wall displays to be evident in the spoken and written words of the children and in their attitudes towards each other and their community.
- Children understand what equality and equity mean and can recognise where they exist and how to respond if they don't.
- Children have the confidence to challenge prejudice and discrimination where they see it.
- All members of the school community will feel valued and respected; race, ethnicity, gender, disability and sexuality are never judged and are always celebrated.

12 Empowerment

Chapter overview

This chapter rounds off the final section of the book by directly addressing the values that, as serious practitioners of wellbeing and character, we would like to see our children possess, cherish and enact as they move through and beyond the primary phase of their education.

Areas discussed

Learning opportunities and activities

Assembly theme

Having taught our children to know themselves, to know others, to look after their peers and adults, to respect diversity, to earn trust and to show responsibility, where do we go from here?

We empower our children.

We empower them to use what they have learned about themselves and about the skills of how to lead, how to be empathetic and how to support their communities. We need to do so because our young people are the future teachers, medical staff, public servants and, dare I say, politicians of the future. Teaching children how to trust, how to respect and how to be safe isn't a box-ticking exercise, but a life skill and ultimately a metacognitive process, where children will use and apply what they know about character and wellbeing as they grow and as they encounter different challenges.

By now, having worked through the themes of earlier chapters, teachers should have equipped children with the tools by which they can drive forward and apply what they have learned and begin to demonstrate their capacity to be good citizens in primary school and as they move on to new environments. If the children apply the principles they have learned, alongside the values their school places emphasis upon, they will have a range of tools in their toolkit to call upon as they meet new challenges and face obstacles and barriers, both in their academic and personal development.

Values matter because values determine who we are. We have all in our lifetimes experienced a range of emotions and actions of others that have either benefited us or caused a problem, leading us to re-evaluate our friendships, connections and relationships. We have all been lied to on occasion, but this is counterbalanced by our experiences of honesty. For every moment of heartbreak, an event that is heart-lifting fills that void. For each time we are treated badly, we look for the positive interactions that give us comfort and respite.

Values in the wider curriculum

In my last school, like many others, we were inspired by the Values Based Education work of Jane and Neil Hawkes (see www.valuesbasededucation.com). By building a cycle of values, chosen by the staff and reflecting the vision, ethos, context and nature of our school, we established a pattern, repeating every two years, that enables values to be embedded in the language of the whole school community and which grows with the children. Detailed below, some of the values are not unique to our setting, but they do reflect the knowledge my colleagues have of the community in which we work and the aspirations we have for our children.

The titles for each value are abstract and open to multiple interpretations. This was a deliberate decision because, as the children become more mature and aware and as the relationships they have with their peers and adults develop, their interpretation of each value will change over time. For example, 'love' will be encountered in Reception and then Years 2, 4 and 6. Whilst ultimately concerning feelings, the spiral nature of the values cycle will mean that there are different questions, emotions and reactions as each topic is revisited. There are also many opportunities for crossover between values, as they are not intended to stand alone – the link of 'respect', 'friendship' and 'loyalty' to the value of 'love' being one example.

Introduced at the beginning of each month in a whole-school assembly, the opening slide is always a reminder that a value is something that guides our behaviour and thinking. By using both of those terms, the message is clear that values are there for every part of the day, in class and on the playground. With all the children and the whole staff in attendance, it is clear that the values are for the whole community, not just for children. The assembly allows for the vocabulary of values to be shared and modelled, so that it becomes embedded in the language of the classroom and the playground. At least one classroom lesson each month is based on the appropriate value, often accompanied by a homework project over a half-term break to engage families too. At the end of the month, each class then chooses their 'values champion', who is recognised and rewarded in the celebration assembly. By the constant drip-feed of the vocabulary of values into every opportunity, the ethos and relationships in the school are fuelled by the language being part of everyday discussion.

The table that follows shows our cycle of values month by month:

	Year 1	Year 2
September	Positivity	Hope
October	Independence	Self-worth
November	Forgiveness	Compassion
December	Caring	Sharing
January	Acceptance	Loyalty
February	Love	Respect
March	Perseverance	Friendship
April	Responsibility	Patience
May	Honesty	Fairness
June	Collaboration	Trust
July	Pride	Courage

The values were placed carefully and appropriately, in many cases to mirror each other in the succeeding year, but there is a strong interrelationship between them all, as our assemblies make clear.

- **September: positivity and hope**
  Deliberately placed at the beginning of the school year, the value of positivity is about new beginnings for our new arrivals and also for those children working with a new teacher. Taking the positive aspects from the previous year, and not dwelling on any negative feelings or emotions, can set an upbeat, but genuine, tone for the year ahead. Hope begins the alternating years, similarly building upon targets and ambitions for the year ahead.
- **October: independence and self-worth**
  The October values can cover the youngest children becoming more independent in making the break from home, to the oldest showing their independence in travelling to school on their own and making safe choices in the use of mobile phones and in friendship groups. It has also allowed for child-friendly discussions on Scottish independence and Brexit. Self-worth mirrors independence, in that we encourage children to be confident in their own abilities and talents, something to nurture and celebrate through their school life, in particular as a way of challenging peer pressure.
- **November: forgiveness and compassion**
  Placed in November, an obvious link to Remembrance Day is made here. Both of these themes lend themselves perfectly to the making of genuine apologies for any unacceptable conduct: what are we apologising for, why are we apologising and what are we going to do to prevent this in the future. The value of compassion is tightly linked to empathy and to authentic feelings; authenticity and lip-service are terms children would find hard to understand, but using the vocabulary of a restorative approach and how another person might feel can add a powerful impact to such discussions.
- **December: caring and sharing**
  Both purposefully placed to coincide with Advent and the Christmas season, the emphasis on giving, empathy (continuing from November) and thinking of others often manifests itself in a 'shoebox appeal', where gifts are sent to children abroad, or a 'Reverse Advent Calendar', where contributions support the local community, in particular the food bank, where toys and games are much appreciated by those families in less economically viable circumstances.
- **January: acceptance and loyalty**
  Here we begin the New Year with a strong emphasis on diversity and how we might respond to discriminatory words or actions. Accepting difference, which covers race, gender, sexuality and disability, as well as understanding

alternative viewpoints, is a recurrent theme that many of our other values address, but a focus in this month drives the message home. Loyalty is a robust ally to acceptance, emphasising how, as a community, we stand by and stand up for each other in the face of behaviours we consider to be wrong, rather than be a passive observer.

- **February: love and respect**
  St Valentine's Day is a link to an understanding of the notion of 'love', which with careful thought can take children beyond the giggly phase that this time of year often results in – particularly in Year 6 as hormones take over – to allow for consideration that 'love' doesn't always mean a loving relationship, and that we can express love as a sign of respect as well as affection. Respect and love are closely linked, and this month represents an excellent time to pursue elements of the RSE curriculum in terms of healthy and respectful relationships.
- **March: perseverance and friendship**
  Two divergent values come up in March, though there is a link in that true friendship survives the test of time and the obstacles that are often thrown in the way. Perseverance, or resilience, supports academic progress in dealing with other approaches to challenge. The friendship assembly can at times link to supporting our friends during bullying incidents and to standing up for what is right.
- **April: responsibility and patience**
  Often coinciding with the Easter break, this is often supported by a holiday project. Children show their responsibility through a litter-pick, supporting a vulnerable elderly neighbour with shopping or considering ways in which they can show responsibility suitable for their age. Patience is often linked to planting of seeds and not expecting instant results or outcomes.
- **May: honesty and fairness**
  Well into the summer term, this pair of values supports honesty and fairness in sports and games, especially as the finer weather allows the children onto the playing field and they invent their own games. May also often coincides with local and national elections (until December 2019 threw a curveball at this), which allows an obvious link to fair conduct of voting procedures and of the honesty of those seeking our support. It also allows for a mature discussion of the phrase 'It's not fair!' and how we might seek to express our feelings if we feel unfairly treated.

- **June: collaboration and trust**
  Both values again marry together this month with a sports theme, coinciding with sports day played as a team, so emphasising the importance of valuing all contributors to the collective effort, not simply the faster runners and strongest throwers. Points for fair play and showing sporting conduct as a spectator add to this value. Trust, as Chapter 9 suggests, is a multifaceted value, but here we talk about trust with a view to transition to secondary school and the next year in primary: who we can trust and demonstrating trustworthy characteristics ourselves.
- **July: pride and courage**
  The final value of the year celebrates the achievements of the year just gone, emphasising a sense of community by sharing what went well. For some children, the tiny steps they make mean the world to them, though another might see this as less significant; it is this other who will be encouraged to appreciate the small things. Likewise, courage celebrates the courage of moving forward, as well as the courage of facing the challenges since the previous September.

British values

Is there anything uniquely British about fundamental British values? Arguably, what we regard as British values are actually universal, much like the values outlined above. What is true is that in some parts of the globe, values such as respect for democracy, diversity, freedom of speech and respect for the law are very different from what we might experience in the United Kingdom. In fact, the fundamental aspects of each of these values is universal because they represent how decent-thinking human beings would act, rather than reflect the belief systems of a particular national identity or its government.

A notion of 'Britishness' is hard to define. For some, queueing politely is a typically British behaviour, but for others celebrating the National Health Service or making an extravagant show of patriotism might show their sense of national identity. Values, though, are about behaviours and attitudes as much as identity.

Nevertheless, British values are important and have a place in our schools, not because Ofsted might be interested in them, but because they do form part of a broad coverage of character development, which we have covered in the chapters on trust, diversity and representation. In considering values as something we hold dear in our society, we should think beyond the school gates and use the knowledge and skill of the wider community to show the children what these values are like in real life.

The five British values are:

- **Democracy:** Invite local councillors or your local MP to speak to the children. Encourage the asking of challenging questions, such as 'What does a member of parliament do?' or 'How can you help my family with this issue?'. This will show the children what democracy looks like in action, not simply as an election process. It brings the notion of accountability of public servants to the attention of children.
- **The rule of law:** Children will be familiar with rules, and they might start to question why we have certain rules in school and in society. The councillors or the MP might be able to talk about how and why laws and rules are made; police officers and magistrates can show how they are enforced. A visit to a magistrates' court is a valuable citizenship experience for older children in Key Stage 2.
- **Individual liberty:** This concerns the rights of citizens to make choices in regard to the aspects of their life beyond government control, including the freedom of speech and the right to make choices about education, faith, lifestyle and work. Inviting representatives of different community and faith groups can be used to inform the children about identity and many of the misconceptions regarding religious dress and the choices around this. Individual liberty can also raise the issue that people make choices that others may not like, but that we should respect choices that are within the law.
- **Mutual respect and tolerance of those of different faiths and beliefs:** Acknowledging and celebrating all the festivals that the school community has promotes understanding of the significance of these in the lives of our families. Diwali, Holi, Eid, Chinese New Year and Hanukkah should have as much of a place as Christmas and Easter. Teaching about the real-life experience of people who have been subjected to discrimination, such as the first arrivals on the Empire Windrush, through diaries, fiction and drama can powerfully illustrate why mutual respect has its place in our values.

The values of *The Wellbeing Toolkit*

Readers of my previous work will know that I based staff wellbeing on values, developing a principled and strategic approach to looking after the school staff, rather than a sticking-plaster and reactive quick-fix attitude. To be serious about looking after the wellbeing of their pupils, leaders need to be taking care of their staff, and vice versa; the two go hand in hand and cannot be separated. Jaded and unhappy teachers will not shape the untroubled and carefree children we might imagine; tension builds pressure, stress feeds anxiety and short tempers undermine confidence. Wellbeing needs to be in equilibrium for staff and pupils, hence returning to the values of my past volume. Here are some suggestions for putting each of the values from *The Wellbeing Toolkit* into action for children's wellbeing.

Celebration

We discussed the value of reward in an earlier chapter. Reward in itself doesn't build character, and the expectation of a reward does not build resilience; rather it resembles a short-term carrot and stick method, with little benefit to either part in the longer term. Reward itself needs to be earned, which means it has to have meaning and some kind of measurable value. Consistency and reliability are at the core of any reward system, but equally, reward needs to have a place in our strategic thinking. We would benefit from a reminder about the SMART acronym here; rewards should be:

- **Specific:** What does your school reward? Behaviour for learning? Children working to, or beyond, their capability? Do you reward children for doing what they should be doing?
- **Measurable:** Can children see how well they are doing? Does a visible system of reward enable children to see how they are acknowledged and how they are being challenged?
- **Achievable:** Whether building up to earning a certificate for a number of merits or one for a particular piece of work, can every child in the class or school do this?
- **Realistic:** Whilst maintaining and not sacrificing consistency and high expectations, are the reward systems in place reflective of the profile of your pupils? Do they allow the children an equal opportunity to be recognised for their achievements and attainments?
- **Time-specific:** A term, a half term or a week is a long time in the life of a child. Does your system allow for each child to be recognised in some way in a specified time frame? How does the child who waits until June for their recognition feel whilst others are rewarded in the first weeks of the academic year?

Rewards need to be equitable and part of the reward system is the celebration aspect to it. Affirmation from peers, adults in school and parents is an important protective factor for our young people. Authentic and empathetic understanding of how well a child has done, shared with the class, can support an agenda of equality of opportunity. We want nobody left behind in learning, so equally we should never leave anyone behind in acknowledging their achievement.

Consider how you celebrate what the children do. Effective celebration isn't through stickers and certificates, though they do have a role to play; intrinsic reward can provide a positive boost and extrinsic reward is more tangible – both, though, need to be meaningful. Celebration is also emphasised through the whole-school assembly, display boards, the school website and social media, and by the children's responses to each other. A child who independently congratulates others for doing well understands the value of celebration.

Collaboration

The children's experience of primary education is where teamwork and a notion of working for and working with each other can be established. The staff in your school will thrive on a culture of strong teamwork and the children will see this, particularly in Early Years, where there is a larger team of adults than elsewhere in the school. Such an early example of adults working together provides a model for the children, one that can be reinforced and embedded through collaborative play, turn-taking and problem-solving activities from an early age. Again, school culture counts for much here; seeing adults visibly working as a team has a positive impact on the teaching environment.

There are multiple opportunities for the children to work collaboratively in school. I believe it is important here not to use this simply as a way of organising learning. Group work is sometimes a maligned or celebrated practice depending upon your perspective, but in terms of character development, being able to work in a group, to develop social interaction and to accept the views of others need to begin at the outset of the children's time in school and be initiated through their continuous provision.

Respect

Respect should be earned and not demanded, but we need, as a starting point, to show that we are a respectful school, with high expectations of that respect being mirrored. These values are communicated through the perception parents have of the school. It requires a presence in the community from the headteacher and the senior leadership team, a presence that is communicated not just from our physical proximity to the parents and children each morning, but through the manner of communication and discourse with them, by letters and email, assemblies and other core school events, such as plays and sports days.

Respectful schools will know their communities and know their children, and in my opinion, the way we show the children the greatest respect is in how we plan for the whole range of learning opportunities, academic and pastoral, that they are going to experience. Planning for their reading, writing, mathematical and creative work should be a given, but so too should be preparing for the pastoral care they will receive, and this applies to all pupils. Respect does not come from an 'I'm the teacher' perspective; this only drives fear and a shallow token of appreciation. Genuine respect is driven by true inclusivity and never seeing any child or family feeling that they are on the margins of school life but that every one of them is valued and cared for.

The cyclical approach to values as suggested on page 178, returning every two years to a specific value, yet also keeping it in the school vocabulary and on everyone's agenda, means that there is a consistent dialogue about each one. Respect has always been an especially powerful one, particularly when linked to the power of words. Though often used, the inauguration address of President John Fitzgerald Kennedy, 'Ask not what your country can do for you – ask what you can do for your country', can be turned into 'what you can do for your *school*', with a sense of service rather than for extrinsic motivation. In short, this encourages respectful behaviour.

With high expectation of respectful behaviour, this becomes embedded in school culture: applause in assembly for every achiever, respect for the environment, respectful behaviour to all staff at all times and that respect returned to children.

Trust

Trust is already covered in depth in Chapter 9, but from the perspective of values and empowerment, if a school that trusts its teachers has effective teacher wellbeing, then by extension there should be the same trust shown in its children. A curriculum designed to promote trustworthy conduct, to identify what trust looks like and to respond appropriately when trust is broken is a curriculum that values the wider learning opportunities that the children in the school have.

Children will be empowered when they are trusted. Trust means not having to micromanage day-to-day activities and routines. Of course, there are going to be children who leave coats on the floor and forget to hand in homework; does it take a harsh lecture or a polite reminder that children are trusted to do these things without being policed? Again, we return here to the importance of relationships in the school; good relationships will see relatively minor matters dealt with by sound classroom management, but where the relationships aren't as positive, such issues escalate unnecessarily.

Giving opportunities to lead, as referenced in Chapter 10, demonstrates that a level of trust brings with it responsibility and recognition. Trust is earned and respected by good leaders, but is also returned through listening and responding and by being able to balance pride and humility. If our school teachers and leaders are able to demonstrate these characteristics, the organisational trust filters down to the children and the wider school community.

Support

My writing for school staff advocated a 'sideways-in' model of wellbeing leadership, one where everyone is a potential leader and wellbeing initiatives and policy aren't imposed from the top or forced up from below. Instead, every member of the staffing community contributes, is valued equally and is supported in the same manner and with the same fairness as each other. Could this model be replicated with the children?

It can, and it is probably easier to do so than with adults, given the right conditions and the culture where support is not only offered without judgement, but asked for without fear of embarrassment or marginalisation. This draws together themes from earlier in the book: respect for diversity, trust, care for each other and leadership. Above all, though, is the openness of the school and the importance for the children of being able to talk about what they feel, what they are going through and how they are coping with their circumstances.

The period of recovery from the pandemic is a startling revelation as to why this is needed. For all the talk of how there is no crisis of mental health and of how academic catch-up is the priority, on the basis, it seems, of guesswork rather than any quantifiable measurement, substantial periods away from friends, the classroom and the familiarity of working with teachers and teaching assistants have had an impact upon our children. They missed social interaction, yearned for games and play, and for the chance to mix with younger or older classes. This too, with a regime of handwashing, 'bubbles' and rotas, has left children needing to catch up on their social and emotional interactions.

By emphasising support as a value and by relating it to the use of positive language and positive feedback, almost by using an approach that as teachers we might have from coaching, we can encourage even the youngest children in the language of support. Allowing their interpersonal and relationship skills to flourish can further encourage the children's empathetic development. Successful classroom modelling of supportive language will demonstrate the expectations that adults have. The 'positivity feedback sandwich', used with adults so effectively, also has a place with the children, the point for development being made between two other aspects that worked well. It takes time to embed, but the return is worth the effort.

Perseverance and resilience

'Be the best that you can be!'

Whilst a laudable aim with high expectations, having a display with this, or a similar title, means little without substance. We can all make a display with words from Malala Yousafzai, Nelson Mandela or any number of politicians, sportspeople or minor celebrities who can punch out a half-decent motivational quote. Having role models and aspirations needs balancing with reality, and whilst we would never puncture any dreams for the future, resilience addresses the here and now, as the primary school is the foundation of what the children will achieve in years to come.

Resilience is discussed within Chapter 9 as a support for trust, but built into the values statement of the school, exemplified in class and included within having high expectations, it can be used as an effective motivator for the children. The language adults use, if it is consistent and encouraging, can drip-feed into that of the children. Modelling improvement and development, going back to errors and trialling how and why they might have gone wrong, demonstrates personal qualities that disabuse the notion of instant gratification or rushing through a task. I am reminded of an episode during teacher training. Our lecturer was discussing poetry and recounted an episode with a well-known children's poet, who had been asked about his writing process and proceeded to show several drafts of one of his poems. Substantial changes could be seen within the early pieces, but the published one wasn't the final draft but one from a few places behind. He explained that any changes he made after that point didn't change the quality of the work and were no more than superficial. This is an excellent example, alongside the often used 'Austin's Butterfly' of improvement through practice, patience and perseverance (Models of Excellence, undated). For those unfamiliar with this, Ron Berger takes the butterfly drawn by a child called Austin, who was then a first-grade student, and through specific critique over six drafts shows how Austin is able to produce a final work of high quality.

Courage

Bravery in leadership means challenging myths and standing up for what is right for our school. Courageous decisions involve challenging what might be seen as accepted norms. Courage also requires the challenging of negative language and discriminatory and bullying conduct, and standing up to behaviours from adults that others might be wary of confronting and might bury their heads in the sand to avoid.

Empowered courage from our children embodies exactly the same expectations. It is the empowered child who will tell a bully that their conduct is wrong, or at least involve an adult, rather than standing by and facilitating that behaviour. For every lesson about racism, gender discrimination and respect for disability, it takes a brave child to put their foot down and say what is wrong. As a value, courage requires us to teach not only right from wrong, but also how to question and to take issue with it in a way that is polite, appropriate yet assertive.

Showing courage demonstrates character. Through a diet of modelling, role play and sometimes conversations about incidents, conflicts and disagreements, we can enable our children to be brave, to stand up to bullying and negativity, and to state clearly what is right. Standing up to such conduct is a measure of character and a clear indication of the value children hold for the wellbeing of others.

Empathy

Empathy is the ability to experience and relate to the thoughts, emotions and experience of others. Children may often confuse this with sympathy, easily enough done without the knowledge of what empathy actually is. Being kind and feeling sad or sorry for someone are positive traits, but are only a starting point for developing empathy. As the children grow, kindness isn't sufficient and can be misplaced; should a child feel sorry for someone who has done something wrong and is upset because they have been told off?

Empathy grows alongside emotional intelligence, which cannot grow from a knowledge base but from foundations of exemplary conduct. It isn't 'being nice' because 'niceness' doesn't build relationships in the future; in fact, it could be a sign or cause of vulnerability. Artificial intelligence is sometimes able to trump emotional intelligence, if excessive screen time negatively affects the language and behaviour of children. Empathy therefore requires a rich vocabulary base as its exemplar, modelled through stories and role play. The teaching of the language of emotions, particularly through reading and through appropriate opportunities for coverage in the wider curriculum, gives context to empathetic words and phrases: how someone feels after being called a name; expressing frustration at a perceived failure in a design technology model or in colour mixing; a suitable description for the lived experience of children in a Victorian workhouse.

Just as with an empathetic response from an adult, the acknowledgement of an issue and the response to it are key to a child's understanding. Take the use of discriminatory language. Whilst it is clearly wrong, needs an appropriate sanction, and should be recorded and reported to parents, think also of this as a teaching opportunity. Why is it wrong? How does it make someone feel? What can be done to prevent this in the future? This is not the language of conciliation, but is firm and fair.

As a school, an empathetic approach should be employed across the community, be modelled through daily interaction, lessons and assemblies and be in the fabric of the school. The way children speak to each other, respond to adults and deal with different levels of challenge will show the depth of empathy and the place it has in our curriculum.

Time

Time, as was referenced in *The Wellbeing Toolkit*, isn't a value, but in itself it has value. It is arguably the most precious thing we have. So, if time is valuable, do we teach our children how to use it effectively? Do we make use of our time in the classroom daily and weekly to share the essentials of wellbeing and character, of the pastoral and caring aspects of the curriculum? Is time celebrated for its worth, or do we watch the clock to the next break and the end of the day?

Actually, as teachers, we are always watching the clock, for the deadlines of registers, getting to assembly on time and dismissing children at the appointed hour at the end of the day. We have all been frustrated at the child taking five minutes to write a title, to find a pencil or to begin working. All these, however, are matters of class management.

To give time its value and its place, we show the children that we take the time for them. When we sit by the child struggling with a fraction calculation, we don't give them a nominal 30 seconds before moving on elsewhere; we give them the appropriate time that they need. It may be the case that those 30 seconds, or less, are sufficient; but it may be that more time is needed for a particular child or group. The point is that this is what we do as teachers, but think beyond the learning and the lesson and it exemplifies the caring and thoughtful ethos that we would wish to see our children replicate. Take the time with the children, and this model is one for the patience we wish them to show elsewhere.

Such modelling can also be seen elsewhere: the midday supervisor who gives the same child a few minutes each day over a week or so to sound out their fears, worries or other problems; the headteacher who steps out of a meeting to solve a lunchtime quarrel; and the teacher who diverts from the lesson to address a crucial point of concern or interest. This shows that there is an appreciation of time that sits beyond the timetable.

Suggested learning opportunities and activities

Unlike previous chapters, there will not be activities suggested for each phase in school; instead, I propose a form of assessment. This is not a test, a timed exercise to add stress to teachers and worry to children, or anything that requires us to say that a child is working 'at expected standard' for their wellbeing and character. Instead, I suggest something that is simple and can be repeated annually, or more frequently if you wish, at the beginning, middle or end of the school year.

Essentially, it is the same activity from EYFS to Year 6, but what the children bring to it will change in content, comprehension and depth as they get older. The 'role on the wall' will be familiar to many of us: an outline of a human figure on a large sheet of paper or, for individuals, the same outline on A3 or A4. The task is simple: to ask what a person who has good character and an appreciation of values shows in their language and conduct. On the inside of the figure, the children show what they believe they demonstrate, and on the outside, what they wish to work towards or what they think others will show.

The youngest children may draw pictures and require an adult to scribe for them. As the children become more confident in their expressive language, illustration will give way to the written word, to greater detail and greater reflection. Where values are strongly embedded, reinforced through language and part of the school culture, the children will find this task easier to complete.

The assessment? This comes from comparing what they have done with the years before. This comparison should be made by the children themselves, in peer groups and in discussion with their adults. Keeping a folder for each child, which may take a little space, will provide a powerful demonstration of how well each has embraced the values of the school and has been empowered in their character development. It's simple, but highly impactful.

An empowerment and values assembly

Similarly, I will not provide a script or template for this assembly, because this one is about celebration and recognition, and will be taken entirely from the work of your school. The context here is in relation to the end of the term, the end of the academic year, of closure, of goodbyes and of reflection. Are your end-of-year assemblies contrived affairs with stiff and awkward handshakes, rehashed speeches, dated certificates and dusty trophies? Or do they celebrate and embrace the spirit of the school and the children who make it live and shine?

A values assembly could include the following:

- a reminder of what a value is: something that guides our attitudes and behaviour
- examples of the value being acted out, from both adults and children
- examples of the behaviour being demonstrated outside school, involving parents and the wider community
- inspirational stories relating to the value (picture books are excellent for this)
- appropriate songs for the children to learn promoting the value
- awards to recognise the value being led and lived.

If we talk of empowerment, amongst the awards chosen by staff, make sure there is a place for some chosen by the children, recognising the skills, attributes and character of their peers. Ensure too that the children have a chance to speak, to proclaim themselves, to celebrate their memories and to express their thanks.

End-of-year assemblies, especially for our Year 6 leavers, are a powerful means of showing the school community the quality of their character, their personal values, and their standing and integrity as young citizens.

These assemblies also celebrate the values that the school holds and that unite the school community, regardless of the challenges that befall it through the course of a school year. Use every opportunity to echo these values and to recognise that they are held dear by all: children, parents and staff.

Success criteria: What does a school that prioritises pupil empowerment and values look like?

- Values don't exist as a message on the wall or on a website banner. They are obvious, because they are there for all to see. Children act those values out, in the way they speak, interact and take pride. This can be seen by all visitors, not just those with a clipboard.
- Values strengthen a school community, enabling children to deepen and build their relationships with each other and with others outside of school.
- Values are known by the children, not by rote but by experience. Children show that they are empowered to use the language and experience of values in how they support their own and others' wellbeing, how they address something they know is unjust and how they take pride in their place in the school and its community.

Conclusion

As this book was being written, school communities were facing possibly the greatest challenge that has been known in recent times. Many teachers, school leaders and educationalists have questioned the purpose of education in light of the difficulties resulting from the pandemic and the pressures arising from decisions made in Westminster.

A second and then a third lockdown, bubble closures, a wholesale shift to online learning with all the pressures and tensions brought by having enough devices and reliable connectivity; the wellbeing and character of children, parents and teachers alike have been put to the test, and stretched to, and maybe beyond, the limit. It is those people with the ingrained sense of values that wellbeing and character entail who will have emerged from this modern crisis with their integrity enhanced and their consciences clear. Wellbeing and character have never mattered more than they do as we emerge as a nation and as a society from the impact of an invasive, insidious yet invisible foe, which has changed in the minds of many of us what 'normality' looks and feels like.

If you are reading this as a teacher, school leader or governor, do you refer to 'my school' or to 'our school' in your conversations? The school isn't your school – sorry to burst that bubble – it is our school, the community's school. The community has lent the school to us for the duration of our tenure and we would do well to remember this, and to remember that, when we hand it back, it should be in a happier and healthier state than when it was loaned to us. Schools thrive on the relationships that are generated by the culture within, by the interactions between the children, staff and parents, and by the underlying ethos that the school leaders have laid down and driven through their determination, attitude and behaviours.

This book is entitled *The Wellbeing Curriculum*, but making a curriculum is a contextualised as well as a creative process. Wellbeing and character have generic features, observable in many schools, but the context of each will be different, defined by the socio-economic and cultural diversity of its community, of its children and of its staff. Our wellbeing curriculum, alongside and astride our academic curriculum, should be the priority of all of us and must be created through a collegiate and collective approach to give it status and meaning.

Schools are judged by academic progress, by the scores the children reach at the end of Year 6, by the numbers of children working at the expected standard or beyond. If any of our children acquire celebrity status in the future and are asked about their most influential teacher, they are less likely to talk about the experience of reaching the expected standard and more so about the teacher who taught the value of empathy, the place of trust, the power of respect and how to persevere. The leaders of the future will rely on a broad range of knowledge and a diverse assortment of skills, including life skills, in charting the path of their organisation or their country. Those core life skills will be determined by their commitment to wellbeing and by the depth of their character.

The Wellbeing Curriculum has addressed three broad themes. In evaluating whether the children have met an 'expected standard' for wellbeing and character, they need to know themselves, be self-aware and make appropriate choices for their own and others' health and welfare. The way that children know others shows that they are aware of the impact they have on society, through their appreciation of friendship, how to deal with issues of bullying and how they are able to demonstrate trust in others as well as be trustworthy in themselves. By pulling together their knowledge of themselves and of how they affect others by their thoughts, words and deeds, children can then show that they have a respect for the diversity of their community, and are empowered to represent and lead others.

An interest in developing wellbeing and character isn't new. In the eighteenth century, the Genevan philosopher Jean-Jacques Rousseau, though in his writing he thought primarily of the schooling of boys, believed that education should develop character and moral sense, and that working in a natural and healthy environment was beneficial to the development of a child. He said in 1762: 'Once you teach people to say what they do not understand, it is easy enough to get them to say anything you like.'

Wellbeing and character are not served by children saying what we want, simply parroting what we say about e-safety and cyberbullying in school only to ignore this at home, or giving an apology with no sincerity so we can tick the apology box on the behaviour record. We want, and need, our children and grandchildren to be honest, to be genuine and to understand what integrity is, because that is how they are going to be truly valued in society. Wellbeing and character fit a school agenda where moral purpose and societal awareness are its heart, its soul and its life.

Further reading

Children's literature to support the teaching of wellbeing and character

I could fill a chapter or more with suggestions for books to share with the children in supporting the themes of *The Wellbeing Curriculum*. Instead I have selected 20 books that I have used in my classes, books that encourage discussion and which have strong moral purpose within their pages. Readers will have many more suggestions, so apologies if I have missed any favourites.

***Krindlekrax* by Philip Ridley (Jonathan Cape, 1991)**
Bullying and friendship, loyalty and honesty, community and resilience: *Krindlekrax* discusses all of these alongside respect for adults and why stereotypes based on physical appearance should be avoided. Bravery and heroism are also shown by the protagonist Ruskin Splinter.

***Holes* by Louis Sachar (Bloomsbury, 2000)**
Read with several Year 6 classes, including one who all sat in gripped silence as I read the final chapters on their last day of primary school, *Holes* is brimming with important issues: race, fairness, equality, justice, bullying, empathy, leadership and belonging. If you choose to watch the film, do so after you have shared the book, as the issues are much more defined in print.

***Skellig* by David Almond (Hodder Children's Books, 1998)**
The arrival of a new and unwell baby sister is one theme that will resonate with some children, but there is also the chance to discuss gender stereotyping, friendship disputes, care for the environment and the benefits of home education.

***The Proudest Blue* by Ibtihaj Muhammad, S. K. Ali and Hatem Aly (Andersen Press, 2020)**

A ground-breaking picture book about religion, sisterhood and identity. Hurtful and confusing words about the wearing of the hijab are faced down with pride and strength. Based on the real-life experience of the author, who wore the hijab as a medal-winning fencer for the US Olympic team.

***Wonder* by R. J. Palacio (The Bodley Head, 2013)**

Inspired by the author's reaction to a child with a facial difference, this book addresses bullying and social exclusion, how bullies can be stood up to and how respect and empathy are values to celebrate.

***Traction Man is Here* by Mini Grey (Red Fox, 2006)**

This delightful picture book challenges superhero stereotypes by having Traction Man use household objects whilst on his adventures. Not all superheroes wear capes; sometimes they have to wear a knitted romper.

***Tusk Tusk* by David McKee (Andersen Press, 1978)**

Less famous perhaps than the *Elmer* series, *Tusk Tusk* features black and white elephants and how their irrational dislike of each other leads to conflict and destruction whilst the peace-loving elephants hid in the jungle. An ideal book to use in discussions around racism and prejudice.

***Where the Wild Things Are* by Maurice Sendak (Harper and Row, 1963)**

Timeless, and applicable across the primary school, Sendak's best-known work addresses behaviour and relationships, anger and solitude in an amusing yet subtly subversive manner.

***Badger's Parting Gifts* by Susan Varley (Harper Collins, 1984)**

I love this book for the sympathetic and sensitive manner in which it deals with death and grief, and addresses how we can remember those no longer with us by their values and attitudes.

***An Emotional Menagerie: Feelings from A to Z* by The School of Life (The School of Life, 2020)**

An alphabetical series of 26 poems, ideal to share, from *Anger* to *Boredom* and beyond. Associating each feeling with an animal allows for discussion of the effects and management of emotions, how they arise and how to deal with them.

***Bill's New Frock* by Anne Fine (Mammoth Books, 1989)**

Bill awakes one morning feeling different and is dispatched to school in a pink dress. This book allows children to discuss how genders could be treated differently, and with older children I have referred to this text particularly in addressing issues of stereotyping in sport or PE.

***The Girl of Ink and Stars* by Kiran Millwood Hargrave (Chicken House, 2016)**

What ostensibly might appear to be a book to support geography, the protagonist being the daughter of the local cartographer, *The Girl of Ink and Stars* can also provide a way into discussing colonialism and imperialist oppression, as well as the values of friendship, trust and making decisions as a leader.

***The Lost Words* by Robert McFarlane (Hamish Hamilton, 2017)**

The 'lost' words relate to aspects of nature that are disappearing and rarely seen. A perfect book to accompany the study of the impact of environmental changes.

***The Iron Man* by Ted Hughes (Faber and Faber, 1968)**

A classic, my well-thumbed copy has been used to discuss friendship, prejudice, recycling and the environment.

***Sad Book* by Michael Rosen and Quentin Blake (Walker Books, 2004)**

Chronicling the grief Rosen felt at the death of his son Eddie, *Sad Book* can be used to acknowledge that sadness isn't avoidable and that complex feelings can be made plain.

***Ron's Big Mission* by Rose Blue, Corinne J. Naden and Don Tate (Scholastic, 2009)**

Ron is Ronald McNair, killed in the Challenger disaster. Telling the tale of his struggle to be able to borrow library books, this book enables discussion of issues of racial discrimination and resilience in the face of rules that are unfair.

***Pig-Heart Boy* by Malorie Blackman (Young Corgi, 1998)**

A powerful story of trust, loyalty, friendship and family values, alongside the subject of organ transplants. One long-lost copy of this book was passed around the class over the course of one year by the power of word of mouth.

***Hello, Sailor* by Ingrid Godon and André Sollie (Macmillan, 2004)**

Matt is waiting for his friend Sailor to return for his birthday, though his neighbours think Sailor will never return. A beautifully illustrated book of hope and friendship, which can be used to discuss the subject of gay relationships.

***Counting on Katherine* by Helaine Becker and Dow Phumiruk (Macmillan, 2019)**

One of the protagonists of the film *Hidden Figures*, Katherine Johnson was the mathematical genius whose skills enabled Apollo 11 to land on the moon and Apollo 13 to return safely. This book is an excellent entry point into the subject of women in science and racial discrimination in the workplace.

***Beegu* by Alexis Deacon (Red Fox, 2004)**

A simple and bittersweet picture book that explores the issues of isolation, loneliness and friendship through the eyes of an outsider.

Useful websites

These websites link to useful resources that can be used in teaching the themes of *The Wellbeing Curriculum*.

Mental health

Place2Be: www.place2be.org.uk

The Anna Freud National Centre for Children and Families: www.annafreud.org

Healthy lifestyles

NHS Change4Life is a useful starting point for healthy recipes:

www.nhs.uk/change4life

Personal safety

Road safety resources from the 'Think' campaign: www.think.gov.uk/education-resources

Safety and citizenship resources from TFL: https://tfl.gov.uk/info-for/schools-and-young-people/safety-and-citizenship

Mizen Foundation – information about the work of Margaret and Barry Mizen: http://mizenfoundation.org

Online safety

LGFL have a wealth of resources for all subjects, but the specific link to online safety is: www.lgfl.net/online-safety/default.aspx

The Breck Foundation resources include teaching about digital resilience: www.breckfoundation.org

Professional development books for teachers

Bethune, A. (2018), *Wellbeing in the Primary Classroom: A practical guide to teaching Happiness*. London: Bloomsbury Education.

Hawkes, N. (2013), *From My Heart: Transforming lives through values*. Carmarthen: Crown House.

Roberts, F. (2020), *For Flourishing's Sake: Using positive education to support character development and well-being*. London: Jessica Kingsley.

Roberts, F. and Wright, E. (2018), *Character Toolkit for Teachers: 100+ classroom and whole school character education activities for 5- to 11-year-olds*. London: Jessica Kingsley.

References

Arthur, J., Kristjánsson, K., Walker, D., Sanderse, W. and Jones, C. (2015), 'Character education in UK schools', http://epapers.bham.ac.uk/1969/1/Character_Education_in_UK_Schools.pdf

Baumeister, R. F. (1992), *Meanings of Life*. London: The Guilford Press.

BBC News (2019), 'Birmingham LGBT teaching row: how did it unfold?', www.bbc.co.uk/news/uk-england-48351401

BBC Newsround (2020), 'Climate anxiety: survey for BBC Newsround shows children losing sleep over climate change and the environment', www.bbc.co.uk/newsround/51451737

Bethune, A. (2018), *Wellbeing in the Primary Classroom: A practical guide to teaching happiness*. London: Bloomsbury Education.

Bush, G. W. (2002), 'National Character Counts Week', https://georgewbush-whitehouse.archives.gov/news/releases/2002/10/text/20021018-9.html

Castro Ruz, F. (2015), 'Reality and dreams', http://en.granma.cu/cuba/2015-08-13/reality-and-dreams

Commission on Race and Ethnic Disparities (2021), 'The report of the Commission on Race and Ethnic Disparities', www.gov.uk/government/publications/the-report-of-the-commission-on-race-and-ethnic-disparities

Cowley, A. (2019), *The Wellbeing Toolkit: Sustaining, supporting and enabling school staff*. London: Bloomsbury Education.

Dalai Lama XIV and Mehrotra, R. (2010), *In My Own Words: An introduction to my teachings and philosophy*. Carlsbad, CA: Hay House.

Department for Education (2019a), 'State of the Nation 2019: children and young people's wellbeing', www.gov.uk/government/publications/state-of-the-nation-2019-children-and-young-peoples-wellbeing

Department for Education (2019b), 'Character education framework', www.gov.uk/government/publications/character-education-framework

Goleman, D. (1995), *Emotional Intelligence: Why it can matter more than IQ*. London: Bloomsbury.

ITV News (2021), 'Black Lives Matter report: system "no longer rigged against ethnic minorities", says review', www.itv.com/news/2021-03-30/overt-racism-persists-but-issues-around-race-less-important--landmark-report

Kellner, D. (1989), *Ernesto 'Che' Guevara (World Leaders Past & Present)*. New York, NY: Chelsea House.

Kessler, R. C., Berglund, P., Demler, O., Jin, R., Merikangas, K. R. and Walters, E. E. (2005), 'Lifetime prevalence and age-of-onset distributions of DSM-IV disorders in the National Comorbidity Survey Replication', *Archives of General Psychiatry*, 62, (6), 593–602.

Models of Excellence (undated), 'Austin's Butterfly', https://modelsofexcellence.eleducation.org/resources/austins-butterfly

NHS Digital (2019), 'National Child Measurement Programme, England 2018/19 school year [NS]', https://digital.nhs.uk/data-and-information/publications/statistical/national-child-measurement-programme/2018-19-school-year

Palacio, R. J. (2012), *Wonder*. London: The Bodley Head.

Roberts, F. (2020), *For Flourishing's Sake: Using positive education to support character development and wellbeing*. London: Jessica Kingsley.

Rose, J. (2009), 'Independent review of the primary curriculum: final report', www.educationengland.org.uk/documents/pdfs/2009-IRPC-final-report.pdf

Rousseau, J.-J., (1762), *Emile: Or on education*.

Seligman, M. (2011), *Flourish: A new understanding of happiness and well-being – and how to achieve them*. London: Nicholas Brealey.

TUC (2021), 'Open letter to the Prime Minister to reject "insulting" report and act on race equality at work', www.tuc.org.uk/research-analysis/reports/open-letter-prime-minister-reject-insulting-report-and-act-race-equality

Vygotsky, L. S. (1978), *Mind in Society: The development of higher psychological processes*. Cambridge, MA: Harvard University Press.

Index